BRITAIN'S MASTER SPY

THE ADVENTURES OF

SIDNEY REILLY

Capt. Sidney Reilly, M.C.

BRITAIN'S MASTER SPY

THE ADVENTURES OF
SIDNEY REILLY

Carroll & Graf Publishers, inc.
New York

First Carroll & Graf edition 1986

Carroll & Graf Publishers, Inc.
260 Fifth Avenue
New York, NY 10001

ISBN: 0-88184-230-3

Manufactured in the United States of America

FOREWORD

By Mrs. Reilly

It is only after long and careful consideration that I have decided to publish the truth about my husband's journey to Russia, and his subsequent capture by the Bolsheviks. What his fate was no one knows. The Bolsheviks have maintained the closest secrecy on the subject, and though, indeed, his name was included in a list of executions published about a year after his capture, and though strong reasons have also been given for supposing that he was actually killed by the secret agents of the Tcheka at Allekul, when he first crossed the frontier, yet I am in receipt of information of a considerably later date, of which the purport is that he is still alive in Russia.

Was Sidney killed at Allekul? Was he actually executed a year afterwards in Moscow? Why was it that the Bolsheviks did not broadcast their triumph to the whole world that they had caught the famous Sidney Reilly, their implacable enemy, who almost overthrew them in 1918, whose work against them the whole world knew, who in 1925 prevented them from raising much needed loans in America? Is he still languishing in a Russian prison without trial or conviction? For my part I sincerely believe that he is still alive.

How the Tcheka shrouds its activities in the most complete obscurity sufficiently appears in the ensuing narrative, where is set forth how it has lured the chief enemies of Bolshevism one by one back to Russia. There were three people whom the Bolsheviks feared beyond all others: Savinkoff, Sidney Reilly and General Koutepoff. Sidney admired both Koutepoff and Savinkoff exceedingly and more particularly the latter; and in this book will be read how they were lured back to their doom by a force which worked with ghastly and occult frightfulness. Whether my husband was the victim of a plot, and walked into a trap which had been set for him, the reader must judge for himself. All I can say is that after his disappearance, first Marie Schultz and then her husband, both associates of Sidney in the Anti-Bolshevik cause, gave their lives in an effort to discover his fate. And both of them undoubtedly were the victims of the Bolshevik provocation agents, who tempted them over the border into that unhappy land where the Tcheka maintains its rule of terror. Nay, I myself received an invitation to go to Moscow to see my husband, and a facsimile of the letter, signed by the notorious Bolshevik *agent provocateur*, Opperput, is included in this volume. All these matters, however, are dealt with in detail in the latter part of this work.

My husband left behind him a great mass of papers connected with his exploits as an agent of the British Secret Service, which are now in my hands. Among them is his complete personal narrative of his part in the so-called Lockhart conspiracy, which forms the first part of this work. Here and there the actors in the story are designated by initials only. The identity of some of them is unknown to me, while of others it has seemed to me to be wisest to preserve the anonymity. Where, however, I have known the names of the persons thus disguised and have been convinced that the publicity could not be fraught with any disagreeable consequences to themselves, I have permitted their several identities to be revealed. Then again considerations of public policy have compelled me to suppress certain facts in Sidney's history. But with these reservations what follows is a complete circumstantial and fully documented account of my husband's career as an agent of the British Secret Service—a story which reads like the wildest dreams of the writers of mystery fiction come true.

Who was Sidney Reilly? Already he is becoming a myth and a legend. All sorts of amazing and fantastic adventures in Germany and Russia have been attributed to him. Everything which passed behind the scenes of the whirl of European war politics has been ascribed by somebody or other to the mysterious Sidney Reilly. Everybody who knows anything of Secret Service operations has heard of him as of a mysterious and potent figure, a man of infinite courage and resource in an amazing variety of disguises. He had become a legend in his own lifetime. A great deal that has been published about him is untrue; though, to be sure, his adventures surpass any fiction. The section devoted to him in Winfried Ludecke's standard work, *Behind the Scenes of Espionage*, abounds in inaccuracies. The work of Saugann, widely read in France but forbidden in England, which affects to be an exposure of British Secret Service methods, is false from start to finish. In typical French style the author represents Sidney as an undergraduate of the University of Oxford, who joined the Secret Service as the consequence of an unhappy love affair. This, in common with the rest of the account, is pure nonsense.

What authentic information with regard to Sidney is at present in the hands of the public? That he was the hero of an amazing series of adventures in Germany during the war, that he was hunted there high and low without being discovered, that he was the English "ace" of espionage, that he visited Litvinoff in prison and went to Russia on a passport provided by the famous Russia revolutionist, that he was appointed to a responsible official post by the Bolsheviks, that he organised the so-called Lockhart conspiracy, that following the fiasco he escaped from Russia by the skin of his teeth and got to the German Naval Base at Reval, that nothing daunted he there resumed his secret service operations, and finally returned to England in possession of the most invaluable information, that he was forthwith sent on another

mission to Russia, where sentence of death had
been passed upon him, that he returned to Russia
again and again, that finally he went once too
often and was captured at Allekul, and that his
fate remains unknown to this day—that sums up
the authentic public knowledge of his activities.
The world knows nothing of Sidney's private life,
of Sidney the ideal husband. It knows nothing of
the romance, the tragedy, the intrigue, the mystery
which forms the background to his amazing adventures. It is my task in the work I have undertaken to give to the public the full story of all these
things, partly in his own words and from his own
papers, and partly from my experiences as the
wife of one of the most amazing men of his
generation.

Sidney George Reilly was born in 1874. His
father was an Irish merchant sea captain and his
mother a Russian. After being educated in Petrograd on purely Russian lines he obtained a post
with the Compagnie Est-Asiatique with whom he
acquitted himself so well that in 1900 he was appointed the chief agent of the company at Port
Arthur. Here he remained for four years familiar-
ising himself with political conditions in the far
East and obtaining a degree of personal influence
and connection which in a few years' time was to
be of the greatest use to himself and to the Russian
government.

In 1904 he returned to Petrograd where he had
been appointed to an important post with the

house of Mendrochovitch and Count Tchubersky at 5 Place de Cathedral de Kazan. This house was the most important firm of Russian naval contractors, and represented in the Russian capital the great Hamburg firm of Bluhm and Voss. At the conclusion of the Russo-Japanese war Messrs. Bluhm and Voss acted as agents for the Russian government in the repatriation of Russian prisoners in Japan and in this connection the experience and personal influence of Sidney Reilly made his services invaluable and enhanced his reputation in Russian official circles. More than this, he was able to use the influence he had gained with the Russian government to place with Bluhm and Voss large orders in connection with the restoration of her navy on which Russia was then engaged, and it may be assumed that his commission was large.

But except for two or three very intimate friends, he never entertained at his own home. Hardly anyone could boast of being his friend. Always a little sombre, serious, elegant, Sidney Reilly was greatly admired at Petrograd, but, naturally enough, the mystery in which he shrouded his personal affairs, made him the subject of innumerable whispered stories and rumours.

Who was he? Nobody knew for certain. On his passport he was described as an English subject, but he neither knew nor cared for the English colony there. Russians regarded him as an Englishman who had become to all intents and purposes Russian. He was known in a dozen European

capitals and was everywhere at home. He wrote
and spoke English, Russian, French and German
irreproachably, but each one, it was remarked
with an accent equally foreign.

In 1909, the year of the exploits of the brothers
Wilbur and Orville Wright, some of the leading
spirits of Petrograd hit upon the idea of forming
an Aeronautical Club. A committee was formed
and the club, under the title of the "Ailles," came
into being. But something more was needed to
give it an impetus. Following a general council
meeting of all its members, a letter was addressed
to Sidney Reilly, asking him to join them. Sidney
Reilly consented, joined them as a respected and
much admired friend, and very soon had become
the leading spirit of the club. For the next two
years all his activities were engrossed in the
"Ailles." He was recognised as a loyal friend, a
good companion, and as a man who dominated his
company.

In the year of the foundation of the "Ailles" he
was appointed to the Council of his old firm, the
Compagnie de Navigation Est-Asiatique. By this
time he was recognised as one of the leading figures
in the Russian commercial world, and circumstances were soon to arise which were to provide
a field for his talents in commercial diplomacy.

Such was his position and reputation when in
1914 war broke out between Russia and Germany,
and at once created a demand for munitions to
which he more perhaps than any other man in

Russia was in a position to attend. He immediately
proceeded to Japan to place contracts for military
equipment in the name of the Banque Russo-
Asiatique. From Japan he went to America and
placed large orders with the chief engineering
firms there. During this period he returned twice
to Petrograd but he was in America when the
news arrived that a revolution had broken out in
Russia, that her continuance of hostilities was unlikely and that in any case her need for munitions
had come to a sudden stop.

Reilly was at a loose end. There was nothing
left for him to do in America and little purpose in
his returning to Russia. The orders which he had
placed were taken over by the British Government
and he himself came to England to put his services
at the disposal of his father's country. His particular value to the British Intelligence Department
became immediately obvious. A man of the greatest courage and resource, he had moreover the
advantage of a perfect mastery of the German language, and in a very short space of time he had
become one of those who undertook the difficult
and hazardous task of entering Germany (usually
by aeroplane *via* the front line) in quest of military information. His services in this direction
were of the utmost value and his exploits in Germany have become legendary, so much so indeed
that it is practically impossible to sift the true from
the false in what has been told of his adventures
there.

He had made a number of trips to Germany whence he had brought back information of greatest value to the Allies when the complete breakdown of Russia and the working there of influences inimical to the Allies led to his being sent to Petrograd to work against the German agents in Russia.

Contents

Illustrations

Documents

Part One
SIDNEY REILLY'S
NARRATIVE

CHAPTER ONE

      "Pass, Comrade Relinsky," said the Lett soldier on guard at the corner of the street.

I passed. The soldier did not trouble to examine my papers. He knew me. I was Comrade Relinsky of the Tcheka-Criminel—a Communist and a Comrade. With the *canaille* in the street it was different. The papers of many of them would be found not to be in order. Fully half of them would be hauled off to the Butyrsky.

I turned into the Tverskoy Boulevard, ruinous, deserted, desolate, strewn with dirt and litter. It was a beautiful day in Moscow—the time Midsummer 1918.

A lean, pitiful scarecrow of an object, starved, emaciated, hungry, was standing at the corner of the Boulevard. He gave me one frightened glance when he heard the Lett address me as a Comrade. Then he shuffled hastily away, pitifully trying to disguise his poor attempt at speed.

It was gloriously warm. The Boulevard was bathed in delightful sunlight. It seemed wrong somehow that the sun should shine and the world go on, when here in Moscow so much shame was being wrought. Was Heaven then indifferent? Could the sun look unblinkingly on the lurid sins of man?

Halfway down the Boulevard I passed another human wreck, an old, old man, with long silver hair and a straggling grey beard. He was crying. His shoulders shook with convulsive sobbing. The shameless tears trickled down his thin, furrowed old cheeks.

"What is the matter, *diedushka*?" I asked him.

"I am hungry," sobbed the old man. "For two days I have stood in the queues and got no food. Lord, have mercy on us, what is to become of us all?"

At the next corner the usual food-queue was waiting. It had been there when I had passed in the morning, three hours before, long, silent, listless, apathetic, like a snake torpid with starvation. The people would come early and line up there, very early, because there was never enough bread to go round. Starvation menaced the city. There were far too many mouths to fill. But the Bolsheviks were steadily reducing the surplus population. Everywhere everything spoke of dearth and stagnation. The peasants got no profit from bringing food into the city. They were rewarded only by a sense of having done their duty. The reward was inadequate. The peasants tilled and sowed for themselves only. Moscow was a city of the damned.

Near the Cheremeteff Pereulok a fitful attempt was being made to clear the litter from the dirty streets. A gang of men and women were working there, men with well-bred, scholarly faces, women dignified and refined. By them, keeping guard, was a workman, covered in bandoliers and with a holster at either hip. They were members of the bourgeoisie; they had been stockbrokers, lawyers, schoolmistresses, when there had been stocks, laws and schools in Russia. Being bourgeoisie they were made to work for the new task-masters. They were tired, emaciated, starving, weary. It was great fun to keep them from the food-queues. A dead horse lay at one side of the road. It had dropped there from sheer exhaustion and starvation, when it had become too weak to go on. It had been left there. The carcass had now been there for several days.

The comrade with the bandoliers and the revolvers called a greeting to me for he knew me. I was Comrade Relinsky of the Tcheka-Criminel. I returned his greeting and passed on, picking my way carefully over the filthy street.

The Cheremeteff Pereulok was in the shade. It was a relief to turn into it from the white glare of the main street. I stopped at No. 3. I turned round. Nobody else was in the street. I was unobserved.

I slipped into the house and mounted the stairs. They were dirty and covered with litter and stunk abominably. The whole house was deathly silent. It might have been deserted—in the hands of the housebreakers probably. As a matter of fact it was a large block of flats, more than two hundred altogether, and all of them were occupied by more

than one family. I came to a halt before a door,
listening and looking very carefully up and down
the stairs before I knocked. The door opened
about half an inch and the point of a nose might
be seen peering round it.

"Is that you, Dagmara?" I asked.

"M. Constantine." There came the sound of a
chain being removed, the door opened, and I
slipped in. The door closed quietly behind me.

I was M. Constantine, Chief of the British
Secret Intelligence Service in Soviet Russia.

.   .   .   .

In the spring of 1918, on returning from a mission, I found my superiors awaiting me with some
impatience. I was instructed to proceed to Russia
without delay. The progress of affairs in that part
of the world was filling the Allies with consterna-
tion. Following the breakdown of Kerenski's abortive administration and the accession of the
Bolsheviks to power Russia had ceased hostilities
against Germany. Germany, relieved of all apprehension in the East, was attacking on the West
with reinforced troops and redoubled ardour.

Of course the part played by Germany in the
Russian breakdown was well known and my instructions were to counter, as far as possible, the
work being done by the German agents, and to
report on the general feeling in the Russian capital. My superiors clung to the opinion that Russia
might still be brought to her right mind in the
matter of her obligations to the Allies. Agents

from France and the United States were already in Moscow and Petrograd working to that end.

After my experiences as an espionage agent in Germany my Russian task seemed safe and easy. I knew Petrograd as a man does know the city in which he has lived from childhood to middle age. I was returning home after an absence of only two years. I had many friends in the city. I knew where I could go when I arrived there. I knew upwards of a score of people on whose co-operation I could implicitly rely. In short the whole mission promised to be the very antithesis of my adventures in Germany, where I had to keep up a perpetual disguise, where any moment might be my last, where often I had no idea where to turn or what to do next.

Accordingly it was Sidney Reilly who arrived quite openly in Petrograd to visit his birthplace and the *cari luoghi* of his youth.

I had not been prepared for the full extent of the change which had come over my birthplace. Petrograd, which once could challenge comparison with any city in the world, bore a ruinous and tumbledown aspect. The streets were dirty, reeking, squalid. Houses here and there lay in ruins. No attempt was made to clean the streets, which were strewn with litter and garbage. There was no police except for the secret police which held the country in thrall, no municipal administration, no sanitary arrangements, no shops open, no busy passengers on the pavements, no hustle of traffic

on the roads. The place had sunk into utter stagnation, and all normal life seemed to have ceased
in the city.

When I had last been in Petrograd in 1915,
food had been scarce and bread queues a feature
of the landscape. Now, in 1918, the bread queues
were still there, but there was no food at all. The
great mass of the people was starving.

It was impossible to obtain any sort of conveyance. Carriages were not to be had for love or
money, if there were any of either at that time in
Russia. I had already determined on my first port
of refuge, the house of an old friend, Elena
Michailovna, who lived in the Torgovaya Ulitza.
It was a longish distance from the Fontanka,
where I had been landed, but I walked there with
as good a grace as I could muster. Everybody I
passed avoided my glance and shuffled by with
obvious suspicion and terror. Petrograd was in a
state of panic. Slowly the atmosphere of horror,
exuded from the very walls and pavements,
seemed to grip at my heart, until I was in a mood
to start at a shadow, and to my mingled embarrassment and amusement I was in a cold bath of
perspiration when finally I reached my goal.

Watching that I was not observed I slipped into
the house. It might have been a necropolis I entered and my footfall awoke a thousand echoes.
I stopped at the well-remembered door and
rapped upon it, my knock reverberating strangely
through the silent building. I had to knock three

times before I heard answering footsteps creeping silently, stealthily, on the other side of the door.

After another pause I knocked again and this time the door opened very silently, very slowly, very little upon its hinges.

The silence was unnerving, but it was Elena Michailovna's voice, which asked in tones of subdued alarm:

"Who is there?"

"It is I, Sidney Georgevitch," said I.

A gasp of surprise answered me. A chain rattled, and the door was opened a little wider.

"You," gasped Elena Michailovna incredulously. "You—back again in Petrograd," and she began to sob quietly with relief.

And thus I came back to Petrograd.

I had already worked out a plan of campaign.

The first thing I did when I had billeted myself was to get into touch with some of the members of my old Petrograd set, whom I thought might be of service. I had to proceed with caution. Some might be fled, others dead, others under suspicion. It was not even impossible that some, despairing of the future, might have joined the Bolsheviks.

However, as it happened, my lucky star was in the ascendant. The man on whose assistance I set more store than on that of all my other potential allies, was immediately procurable. Grammatikoff was not only a scholar and a thinker, but a man of character. He had been long acquainted with me and his loyalty was above suspicion. It was a queer moment when I heard his voice over the wire. Two years had passed since last I spoke to him, and in those two years Russia had been turned upside down. It made our friendship seem immensely ancient somehow, as if we were survivors of a forgotten civilisation.

In pursuance of my policy of appearing in my own person, I fixed an appointment with him at his office and went round to see him openly. Grammatikoff gave me a very graphic and terrible account of the position of affairs in Russia. The new masters were exercising a *régime* of bloodthirstiness and horror hardly equalled in history. The most ignorant and the most vile, everybody who conceived that they had a grievance against society were in the ascendancy. Russia, Grammatikoff said, was in the hands of the criminal classes and of lunatics released from the asylums. Nobody did any work. There was a growing want of all the necessaries of life. People were starving. The vast majority were prepared to rise in revolt, but there was nobody to lead them. The terror of the Tcheka was heavy on every man.

All the higher officials of the Tcheka are members of the Communist Party, and the names of some of them are known. But who are its servants what man shall say? The man who has been your friend from infancy, the woman you love, nay, your parents or your children may be in the service of the Tcheka against you. It is a terrible, a gruesome, a ghastly thing. Nobody trusts anybody any more; no man dare commit a secret even to his bosom friend. Some of its work is done by *provocateurs,* men who deliberately foment counter-revolutionary plots, and when they have engineered a conspiracy, which is just about to burst into open flame, betray it to their masters. The streets run with blood, and one more counter-revolutionary plot is discovered and avenged.

In the foul cells of the Butyrsky at Moscow sit scores of the wretched victims of the Tcheka. The "Investigators" employ every diabolical device, every ghastly torture ever invented by the fiendish ingenuity of man to wring from them a confession or a betrayal. They are held under examination without rest or food until the reason goes, and in their madness they reveal their complicity in plots, real or imaginary, against the Bolshevik power.

Such is the Tcheka, which ministers to the preachers of the foulest and most horrible gospel known in the history of the world. Such are the means by which, unless it is checked and that soon, Bolshevism will master every country in the world. And it can only be checked by an organisation as subterranean, as secret, as mysterious, as ferocious and inhuman as itself.

In Petrograd, however, I was but a bird of passage. The capital of Russia and the headquarters of Bolshevism were located in Moscow, whither I was now ready to proceed. But here an unforeseen difficulty interposed. Travelling by railway between Petrograd and Moscow was only possible on a pass, and passes were forbidden to all but officials. "Divide et impera" was the Bolshevik motto.

In this difficulty I was able to avail myself of Grammatikoff's assistance. Grammatikoff had charge of a fine library, and among the Bolsheviks then in Moscow was the bibliophile General Brouevitch. Brouevitch had approached Grammatikoff with an offer to buy some of his books. At my suggestion Grammatikoff offered, if Brouevitch would secure him a pass, to come to Moscow, bringing me with him. The Bolshevik general was charmed and Grammatikoff and myself set out for Moscow under official favour. And Moscow was a city of the damned.

Something like this, I thought, Hell must be—paved with desolation, filth, squalor, fiendish cruelty, abject terror, blood, lust, starvation. The Bolsheviks were masters of Russia.

A city of the damned. Slowly it sank into stagnation; hoardings went up to cover dust and rubble and ruin, or did not go up and left dust and rubble and ruin naked. There had been looting at first, but now there was nothing left to loot. The rabble had been riotous, full of the lust of blood and destruction. Now the rabble was cowed and frightened, except for the few that were Bolsheviks. Everywhere was starvation, food-queues, that had forgotten to be clamorous, dearth, stagnation. And over all silent, secret, ferocious, menacing, hung the crimson shadow of the Tcheka. The new masters were ruling in Russia.

A city of the damned. Bolshevism, the new bantling of slow time, had been baptised in the blood of the bourgeoisie. Among its leaders were those who had been before oppressed by society —whatever they were, criminals, assassins, murderers, gunmen, desperadoes. The more serious their crimes had been, the heavier the penalties hanging over their heads at the time when all prisoners in the state prisons were released, the greater was their grievance against society and the greater was their welcome to the ranks of Bolshevism. A man who could read and write was eyed askance; the illiterates were obviously of the oppressed, and now their time had come.

The premium put on ignorance among the high Bolshevik officials was of the greatest value to the British Secret Service. Many of my agents operated with passports which were something more than dubious, and which were frequently scanned with an air of great knowingness by Commissars, who could neither read nor write.

The hated bourgeoisie, many of whom had been among the prime movers in the Revolution of the previous year, were put to work for the new masters. There they were cleaning the streets beneath the watchful eye of an armed workman. In each block of flats there had been constituted a committee of servant-girls, yard-keepers, cleaners, porters, who beneath the new banner of Liberty ceased to do any work, and carried off from the flats of their erstwhile masters and mistresses such furniture as they coveted for the better decoration of their own apartments. For furniture, of course, belonged not to yourself, but to the community. At any moment a party of comrades might arrive and make their choice out of your belongings.

Here and there pathetic attempts were made to carry on as if nothing in particular had happened, spasmodic attempts at retaining some of the decencies of civilisation, which flickered precariously for a time, and then—blackness.

And everywhere there was a current of murmuring, of bitterness, of counter-revolution.

The Bolsheviks laid this at the door of the Allied missions. There were still at this time representatives of civilised countries in the City of the Terror. A German Embassy was resident there in charge of Count von Mirbach, and in opposition a British Mission led by Mr. Bruce Lockhart. There was an American Consulate under Poole and a French under Grenard. Furthermore there were Allied agents in the city, an American Kalamatiano and a French de Vertemont. But though I had been informed of their presence I judged it best to keep clear of them, thinking that my mission could be best fulfilled if I worked on my own, and employed the assistance of Russian accomplices only.

Brouevitch received Grammatikoff and myself very graciously. Grammatikoff introduced me by my own name, informing him that, though English by nationality, I had been born in Russia and lived there all my life, and was in fact to all intents and purposes Russian. I corroborated this story and added that I was very interested in Bolshevism, the triumph of which had brought me back to Russia.

Brouevitch listened to this declaration, which after all, was quite true, with great complacency, and in response to my request gave us every facility for studying Bolshevism in its cradle.

Nobody could be more officious on our behalf than Brouevitch. It was he who enabled us to attend a meeting of the Soviets in the Grand Theatre, where Lenin in his address made a revealing distinction between the leaders and the rank and file of the Communist Party.

"The period of destruction is over," said Lenin. "The bourgeoisie is extinct, Korniloff is dead, the White Army has crumbled away, Koltchak has been finally repulsed. We must now begin the construction of the Socialist State. If we have not the Socialist discipline, if we do not construct the Socialist State, the capitalists and imperialists of the entire world will fall upon us. We," said Lenin, with a sweep of his arm embracing all the occupants of the stage at the Grand Theatre at Moscow, "we will have to make our terms, you,"—with a gesture towards the crowded auditorium, where the deputies or the local soviets had their seats— "you will perish."

"You say that the bourgeoisie is extinct," cried Gay, the notorious anarchist, "you say that the reign of terror can stop and the period of reconstruction begin. Well, here is a story: a man was very ill and the doctor said to his wife, 'Madam, we can do no more for your husband. All the evidence of science shows that he will be dead tomorrow.' By chance the lady met the doctor again two years after, and said to him, 'Doctor, my husband is still alive!' 'Yes, you think he is alive,' replied the doctor. 'For you he is alive. For Science he is dead.'"

The reign of terror went on. The bourgeoisie continued to be shot down by the hundred. The Tcheka struck, struck, struck again and again. The streets ran with blood. Of the obscene and ghastly horrors of the Butyrsky, mercifully we can form no estimate.

"All the Bolsheviks are sadists at heart," said to me the last doctor to practise in Moscow.

It soon became obvious that Brouevitch intended to be obliging to the point of embarrassment. We were permitted to go nowhere unattended, and, so that we should not be unduly embarrassed, our watchers had instructions to make themselves as inconspicuous as possible. Wherever we went we were followed. It became obvious that, if I were to carry out the mission on which I was engaged, I must disappear.

It was not difficult for us to find somebody to accompany Grammatikoff back to Petrograd in my place. Moscow was full of people who were anxious to leave it, and our only task was to light on someone who bore a passable resemblance to me. Both Grammatikoff and myself had friends in the city, and could call on assistance from many quarters. Indeed my visits to one or two old friends were known to Brouevitch and the substitution was made with greater ease than might have been anticipated.

When the morning arrived I watched from safe concealment Grammatikoff and the pseudo-Sidney Reilly set off from the station. I knew that hidden eyes were watching them, that unseen spies were dogging their footsteps, and I prayed that they might reach their destination without their secret being surprised. By the greatest good fortune the day was squally and my representative with his nose appearing from a voluminous, if ragged coat, bore a sufficiently close resemblance to me.

Thus I changed my identity and became M. Constantine. M. Constantine's future was mapped out for him. It would of course be unwise for him to visit any of the known friends of Sidney Reilly, but in his pocket he had a letter addressed by Grammatikoff to Dagmara K.

Dagmara was Grammatikoff's niece and, as such, of course, perfectly well known to me, though I had not seen her since before the outbreak of the war. She was now a dancer at the Arts Theatre and shared a flat in the Cheremeteff Pereulok with two other young actresses, the Mlles. S. Now

among the colleagues of these young ladies at the
Arts Theatre was Mlle. Friede, sister of no less a
personage than Colonel Friede, who at that time
was Chief of the Bolshevik Staff in Moscow. It
became obvious at once of what use Dagmara could
be to me and why I wanted an introduction to the
charming Mlle. Friede.

It was no surprise to me to learn that Mlle.
Friede and indeed her brother, the Bolshevik
Chief of Staff, were not Bolsheviks. Most of Moscow was anti-Communist. The town swarmed with
White Russians. Many of them were in the em-
ployment of the Bolshevik authorities. By the
granting of extraordinary privileges, particularly
in the all important matter of rations, the Bolsheviks were endeavouring to increase their member-
ship. People slipped into the Communist Party
very easily. I saw the advisability of becoming a
member myself.

My great purpose at present was of course to
secure copies of those confidential military documents which passed through the hands of Colonel
Friede. And as it happened the Colonel's sister
was not only a close friend of the Mlles. S. but
frequently visited them at their flat in the Cheremeteff Pereulok. These young ladies were entirely
on my side, and it was arranged that I should meet
Mlle. Friede there. The meeting was a great success. When I was sure of Mlle. Friede, I unfolded
my proposition to her, namely that her brother
should secure me copies of all documents which

passed through his hands. Mlle. Friede greeted the suggestion with joy, and assured me that her brother was only too anxious to be able to strike a blow against Bolshevism.

I had one or two surreptitious meetings with Friede, and when we were each assured of the other's *bona fides*, he became my most willing collaborator. All *communiqués* from the Archangel front, from the Korniloff front, from the Koltchak front passed through his hands. All army orders, all military plans, all confidential documents relating to the army fell within his province, and many a copy of a highly confidential document he handled was read in England before the original was in the hands of the officer to whom it was addressed.

The house in Cheremeteff Pereulok was a large place, containing no fewer than 200 flats, and some of these were of the largest size. The flat for example, occupied by the Mlles. S. which was on the third floor, was altogether too spacious for the young ladies who occupied it, and rooms of it were let to two sub-tenants, an ex-Government official and a professor of music. These interesting young ladies had a regular visitor, whom they knew as Sidney Georgevitch, officially described as Relinsky of the Tcheka-Criminel.

What more natural than that the young artistes should be visited by a close friend of theirs, Mlle. Friede, also of the Arts Theatre? The young ladies were apparently very much attached and the visits were of daily occurrence. Mlle. Friede would bring her portfolio with her, and no doubt the young ladies met for the purpose of practising triolets together under the guidance of the music master.

Yes, but portfolios may be made to carry many more things than a pianoforte score. Mlle. Friede lived with her brother in a flat not very far away. Every evening he would bring home copies of the Bolshevik despatches and orders. The following morning she brought them round to the Cheremeteff Pereulok, where they were duly handed over to me.

In fact the flat in Cheremeteff Pereulok was my headquarters in Moscow and Mlles. S., Friede and Dagmara K. were among my most loyal and devoted collaborators.

And thus it was that I was absolutely *au courant* with everything that was happening on all the Bolshevik fronts, and was enabled to get a correct orientation of the political and military position of the *régime*. Some of these *communiqués* were in the highest degree humorous and characteristic, as when the young Red General Sabline telegraphed: "Our canaille has ratted again, and we have been obliged to yield Red Hill."

My own official reports to my superiors in London always took one form. Beneath their national apathy the great mass of the Russian people longed to be delivered from their oppressors. Give Russia a popular government and once more she would show a united front to the Germans. In any case Bolshevism was a far worse enemy than Germany, a hideous cancer striking at the very root of civilisation.

It was pretty obvious that, if they could only be made to co-operate, the anti-Bolsheviks could seize the reins of power with ease. Numerically they were far superior to their enemies. But they were leaderless. The Russians are useless without a leader. Without a leader they will stand and let themselves be slaughtered like so many sheep. I was positive that the terror could be wiped out in an hour, and that I myself could do it. And why not? A Corsican lieutenant of artillery trod out the embers of the French Revolution. Surely a British espionage agent, with so many factors on his side, could make himself master of Moscow?

The armed forces on which the Bolsheviks relied were Letts. The Red soldiers were deserting by hundreds of thousands. But the Letts could not desert. Latvia was in the hands of the Germans. The Letts were the only soldiers in Moscow. Whoever controlled the Letts controlled the capital. The Letts were not Bolsheviks; they were Bolshevik servants because they had no other resort. They were foreign hirelings. Foreign hirelings serve for money. They are at the disposal of the highest bidder. If I could buy the Letts my task would be easy.

Meantime it was necessary for me to travel to Petrograd fairly often, both to carry the despatches

which Colonel Friede brought and to confer with
my friends in that city. Accordingly I requested
Colonel Friede to secure me a pass. The Colonel
advised me to obtain an official post under the
Soviet, as he had done, and gave me, in addition
to the pass, a letter of introduction to Orlovsky,
President of the Tcheka-Criminel in Petrograd,
but like Friede an anti-Communist.

There are two branches of the Tcheka—the political secret police, of which Dzerjinski was the
head, the most diabolical organisation in the history of the world, and the criminal branch answering to the civic police in a civilised country. It
was of this latter that Orlovsky, formerly a judge,
was President, and to his office I went on my
arrival in Petrograd.

It was entering the lion's den with a vengeance,
but there was no help for it. If I was to have a
regular pass to Orlovsky I must go. And accordingly when I returned to Moscow I was Comrade
Relinsky, collaborator of the Tcheka.

Needless to say I was not slow to make use of
my new office. It gave me opportunities, which
were of the greatest value to me and which I
quickly turned to account in securing very valuable information.

Orlovsky was a man of sardonic humour. I remember Grammatikoff's account of his first meeting with Monsieur le President. One day to his
extreme horror he received a summons from the
Tcheka-Criminel. In fear and trembling poor

Grammatikoff presented himself at the offices of the Tcheka, which were situated in the old Ministry of the Interior on the Fontanka quay, and was immediately conducted into the sumptuous apartment of the old Ministry, which had been assigned to the President of the Tcheka-Criminel. The President was sitting at his desk, and a stenographer was in the room with him.

When Grammatikoff entered the President introduced himself with a strong Polish accent as "Veneslav Orlovsky."

Then he dismissed the stenographer and turning to Grammatikoff said in pure Russian:

"Well, Monsieur Grammatikoff, I perceive that you do not recognise me."

Grammatikoff realised that the gentleman before him was someone he knew, but who it was he could not say. The President resembled someone— but who?

"You remember Orloff," resumed the President, "*juge d'instruction* at Vaisovie?"

Grammatikoff was a barrister and had practised in that court. And now he recognised in the gentleman before him the famous *juge d'instruction* in espionage cases. How had he become President of the Tcheka? That was the sort of question one did not ask.

"I know," said Orloff, "that you must go to Moscow, but all travelling between Petrograd and Moscow is forbidden to the ordinary citizen. Here is a return ticket. You will travel as a collaborator

of mine. And now—*au revoir*. Come and see me
again as soon as you return from Moscow."

Grammatikoff and myself thus very simply
solved the extremely difficult question of travelling
between Moscow and Petrograd. We travelled as
collaborator of the Tcheka-Criminel.

On my return to Moscow I proceeded at once
with the organisation of my conspiracy, and the
preparation of the White Russians to wipe out the
terror. I had to be cautious though.

The Tcheka was everywhere and the chances
that I would enlist some of its *provocateurs* into
my scheme were large. It was essential that my
Russian organisation should not know too much,
and that no part of it should be in a position to
betray another.

The scheme was accordingly arranged on the
"Five" system, and each participant knew another
four persons only. I myself, who was at the summit
of the pyramid knew them all, not personally, but
by name and address only, and very useful was I
to find the knowledge afterwards, as I shall have
to show. Thus, if anything were betrayed, everybody would not be discovered, and the discovery
would be localised. The mind shudders to con-
template how ghastly the revenge would be if there
were a complete betrayal.

No less than 60,000 officers, who lived in Moscow, were in the conspiracy and were ready to
mobilise immediately the signal was given. Grammatikoff had been right in saying that the White

Russians were only waiting for a leader. A well-known Tsarist officer, General Judenitch, was immediately to take command of this army. From the outside our nearest assistance would be from General Savinkoff who was hammering away at the outskirts of Russia with one of the counter-revolutionary armies. As soon as the insurrection had proved successful the way for Savinkoff into Russia would be clear and what remained of the Bolsheviks would be between an upper and a nether millstone.

All arrangements were made for a provisional government. My great friend and ally Grammatikoff was to become Minister of the Interior, having under his direction all affairs of police and finance. Tchubersky, an old friend and business associate of mine, who had been head of one of the greatest mercantile houses in Russia, was to become Minister of Communications. Judenitch, Tchubersky and Grammatikoff would constitute a provisional government to suppress the anarchy which would almost inevitably follow from such a revolution.

All this of course entailed a great deal of organisation. Looking back I wonder that in so short a time I was able to accomplish so much. Only two things remained to be done. The most formidable obstacle in our path was constituted by the Lettish garrison, who, as I have explained, were mercenaries in the pay of the Bolsheviks. I must buy their support. Secondly, I must time the rising when both Lenin and Trotzky should be in Moscow. For Lenin and Trotzky *were* Bolshevism. Once they were removed the whole foul institution would crumble to dust, but while they lived there could be no peace in Russia. It was accordingly necessary to our success for us to arrest Lenin and Trotzky at the first blow.

The money was very soon forthcoming for the purchase of the Letts. There was no lack of anti-Communists in Moscow who were prepared to sacrifice their all if necessary to overthrow the horror which was reigning in Russia. In a surprisingly short space of time there were hundreds of thousands of roubles in the bureau drawer in Mlle. S.'s flat in the Cheremeteff Pereulok.

Finally I got into touch with Colonel Berzin, one of the three Lettish commandants. Berzin was a soldier and a gentleman, a sworn foe of Germany and of Communism. If afterwards he revealed to the Bolsheviks certain details of our conspiracy, it was under the stress of tortures too terrible to be borne. I am satisfied that the Bolshevik story that he was from the start one of their provocation agents is a vile scandal.

Berzin came to me, as it were, with a recommendation. He was already co-operating with the Allied Secret Service, with de Vertemont the French agent, and with de Vertemont's American colleague, Kalamatiano. At the time I had not met these two gentlemen, judging it best to keep myself to myself, but I was informed of their activities by Captain Hill, who was attached to the

British Mission and whom in the course of my duties I met frequently in Moscow. Afterwards Hill and myself were to be in several tight corners together and to get out safely. That was when the Mission was under surveillance, when Bruce Lock-hart, its head, was a prisoner, and when Hill was a wanderer in a Moscow grown rabid.

When I had sounded Berzin and entirely satis-fied myself with regard to him, I unfolded some of the details of my conspiracy and asked him whether the collaboration of his Lettish colleagues could be secured. Our meeting took place at the Tramble Café in the Tverskoy Boulevard, and I stressed the money side of the question, promising large sums to the commandants and proportionate rewards to the lower ranks.

Berzin assured me that the task I had set him was easy, that the Letts were full of disgusted loathing for their masters, whom they served only as a *pis aller*. In consideration of my princely proposals he could positively guarantee the future loyalty of his men to me. Thereupon I handed him over some earnest money instructing him to divide it with his fellow commandants. And from that time Berzin dipped regularly into our exchequer.

I had merely to await my opportunity.

Meantime, starvation increased in Moscow. The patient queues waiting in the streets showed faces daily thinner and more emaciated. The comrades did not stand in queues. Not vainly had Lenin differentiated between "We" and "You". Daily the streets grew more dirty and litter strewn. Horses starved and fell exhausted, whipped to the last ounce of energy that was in them. There was nobody to remove the carcases. There they lay putrescent. Civilisation was losing the battle in Moscow, losing disastrously.

The Tcheka raids went on. People would go out in the morning and never return. Or you would visit the flat of the friend with whom you had talked and eaten yesterday, and find it empty, ransacked, desolate. Who were languishing in the terrible Butyrsky? Nobody knew; nobody dared ask questions.

The position of the representatives in Moscow was daily becoming more precarious. When my conspiracy was approaching fruition the German ambassador, von Mirbach, was shot down, assassinated, it was said at the time, by a White Russian who regarded him as the author of the horrors now being enacted in Moscow.

I shall never forget the comments on the crime which appeared in the Allied newspapers. The tone of them, while professing a proper abhorrence of the crime, was laudatory, congratulatory. Now, at last, a misled Russia was returning to a better frame of mind, had discovered who was her real enemy. Germany, Germany was the enemy. At all costs Germany must be brought to her knees.

Gracious Heavens, will people in England never understand? The Germans are human beings; we can afford to be even beaten by them. Here in

Moscow there is growing to maturity the arch-enemy of the human race. Here monsters of crime and perversion, to the fact of whose very existence the delicacy of society decreed for centuries that its very eyes should be shut and its very ears closed, are regnant. Here the foulest, most monstrous and most obscene passions, which have been suppressed and bridled by the common decency of people at large and by the strong hand of a most beneficent authority since civilisation first began, gibber and swagger in the seats of government. Here minds, of the like of which decent people were once not allowed to know, rule and control. Here men, who have been under sentence for nameless crimes, administer with a horrible parody of justice a satiric law. Here criminals of every mentionable and unmentionable kind are preparing an unholy war of revenge against civilisation, which has only lasted by suppressing them. The mental perverts of the world, in the extremity of their rage against the forces which have kept them in chains so long, have openly declared war on everything which the world has been taught to consider pure and right and noble.

If civilisation does not move first and crush the monster, while yet there is time, the monster will finally overwhelm civilisation.

As a matter of fact the Bolsheviks wished to drive the foreign envoys out of Russia. They had been saying for some time that the headquarters of the counter revolution was at the foreign missions. A disastrous fire had occurred at one of the railway stations, in which the Bolsheviks informed us that a quantity of provisions was destroyed. In point of fact the conflagration was started by the Bolsheviks themselves, who had to find some excuse why there should be no food in a starving Moscow. They said that this fire was the work of the French mission.

The Allies themselves were anxious enough to leave Moscow. There was no point in remaining there. The city had sunk into a state of putrescence and stagnation beyond recall. It was fit to excite the disgust of any decent man. The Missions were exposed to the insults of mentally and physically unhygienic commissars. The Consulates were raided more than once and the Allied representatives treated with the grossest indignity and contumely. Infamy was piled upon infamy until at last the missions, after registering an emphatic protest, prepared to shake the dust of Moscow off their feet.

It was arranged that Captain Hill should remain in Moscow to assist me in intelligence work. Though he was my superior in rank, Hill unselfishly placed himself under my command and never could man wish for more gallant and devoted a collaborator. Moreover the American agent Kalamatiano and the French agent de Vertemont were to remain in hiding in the city for purposes of espionage, and it was proposed to me that as chief of the British Secret Intelligence Service in Moscow I should meet de Vertemont and arrange for our future co-operation.

I had an uneasy feeling (such as one frequently gets in dangerous situations, when one's nerves are constantly on the "qui vive") that I should keep myself to myself and not go to the meeting which had already been arranged for me. But in the end I allowed myself to be persuaded.

The meeting took place for safety at the American Consulate, the only one which had not yet been raided by the Bolsheviks. M. Grenard, the French consul, introduced me without naming me to de Vertemont, who of course knew who I was, and then, to my surprise to Réné Marchand (again without naming me) whom he described as a confidential agent of the French Government. And here it was that the uneasy feeling, which had been haunting me all along, became acute. Marchand asked me my name, and I mumbled the first that came to my mind. I do not recall it now, but in his letter, as printed in the *Isvestia*, R. gave it as Rice.

I was by no means favourably impressed with M. Marchand, Moscow correspondent of the Paris *Figaro* though he was, and discreetly drew de Vertemont into another room and arranged with him some details about liaison. To do so I had to disclose to him some details of our conspiracy. The room in which we were was long and badly lighted. In the midst of an animated discussion I suddenly became aware that Marchand had crept

in to the room, and no doubt had already overheard a large part of our conversation.

However there was no help for it now. I could
only hope that my intuition had been wrong.

The organisation of the conspiracy was now
complete. It was arranged that upon the signal
being given, their Lettish bodyguards were to arrest Lenin and Trotzky, and to parade them pub-
licly through the streets, so that everybody should
be aware that the tyrants of Russia were prisoners.
At the same time the provisional army was to mobilise under General Judenitch, and the provisional government be instituted. As soon as affairs
in the city were sufficiently quiet—a matter of a
very few days—an army was to march off to co-
operate with General Savinkoff against the Red
forces which still were in the field against him.
Another force would be despatched to Petrograd
where a simultaneous rising was to take place and
Uritzsky, the head of the Tcheka, to be arrested.
The scheme sounds fanciful enough, but our organisation was now immensely strong, the Letts
were on our side, and the people would be with us
as soon as the first blow was struck.

We had now merely to await the return of
Trotzky, and, as it happened, there was not long
to wait. On the 20th of August Mlle. Friede informed me that in eight days' time there was to
be a meeting of the central committees of the
Soviet in the Grand Theatre. Lenin was to address

them and Trotzky was to give a report of the position on the Koltchak front.

I saw Berzin that same evening and learned that he already had the news. One of the Lettish regiments would in the course of its duty be on guard at the exits and entrances of the Grand Theatre. The meeting might have been arranged for my benefit. I told Berzin that whatever commandant was detached for duty was to choose the men whom he was absolutely sure were faithful and devoted to our cause. At a given signal the soldiers were to close the doors and cover all the people in the Theatre with their rifles, while a selected detachment was to secure the persons of Lenin and Trotzky. The special detachment was to consist of my inner circle of conspirators, with myself at their head. We were to be previously introduced into the theatre by the commandant and to take up our place in hiding behind the curtains. In case there was any hitch in the proceedings, in case the Soviets showed fight or the Letts proved nervous when it came to the point, in case of a thousand and one unforeseen accidents which might intervene, the other conspirators and myself would carry grenades in our place of concealment behind the curtains.

When our plans were completed there came the news that the grand meeting had been postponed for a week. It was to be held on September 6th. I did not mind that. It gave me more time to make my final arrangements. I decided to take advantage of the delay and return to Petrograd, confer with Grammatikoff, and give my final orders.

Incidentally, it would be useful to know what was the attitude of the Letts in Petrograd, and to what extent the organisation had grown there. Berzin would be useful in this matter. He was in touch with the Lettish colony in Petrograd, and I wished to use him for the issue of Lettish proclamations.

I saw him again in the Griboiedov Pereulok and suggested that he should proceed to Petrograd. He was agreeable to set off at once. I gave him my address there and told him to ask for Mr. Massino, the name which, together with the character of a very respectable Levantine merchant, I bore in Petrograd.

On the night of August 28th, Comrade Relinsky, travelling on a pass signed and sealed by Veneslav Orlovsky, President of the Tcheka-Criminel, boarded the train to Petrograd.

Chapter Two

In Petrograd I was Mr. Massino, a Turkish and Oriental merchant. I proceeded at once to No. 10 Torgovaya Ulitza, Mr. Massino's Petrograd address. Elena Michailovna was waiting for me. There was quite a dainty little repast ready, some soup, some fish, a fowl and some cheese, fortified by a bottle of wine, which Captain Cromie had sent from the Embassy. Elena told me that Berzin had been there that afternoon, as he had promised me in Moscow. He had waited about an hour and then gone to see some friends in the Latvian quarter. He would see me on the following day.

That night my sleep was the sleep of a child. Tired! God, how I was tired. But now at last the end for which we had striven was in sight. Berzin had distributed his roubles wisely. One blow and Lenin and Trotzky were our prisoners, Moscow in our hands, and this monstrous abortion, which had crept from the teeming womb of time, was crushed, crushed for ever, its noisome head broken beneath our heel. To-morrow I must see Grammatikoff, hear what progress the Expeditionary Force was making towards Vologda, learn what move Savinkoff was likely to make, send my report to England, and then back to Moscow and be pre-

pared to strike. Although we had not yet reached
the needle point, though the worst was yet to come,
I felt as if the load I had carried for the past few
months was slipping off my shoulders. There's
many a slip, of course, 'twixt the cup and the lip.
But what *could* go wrong? There would be danger
for *us* of course in the Grand Theatre, when the
blow was first struck, but at any rate there was
no possible escape for those monsters against whom
we were to pit ourselves. Myself and my picked
band might die, but with us would die the tyrants
who had made of Russia a charnel-house. Nothing could possibly save *them*. Once they were out
of the way, well there was always Savinkoff and
others of our friends to re-establish the broken and
blood-drenched country.

．　　　．　　　．　　　．　　　．

The dear city, which had been my home during
so many happy years before the war, looked more
ruinous and deserted than ever. The streets were
littered and untidy and after the heat of that
August day stunk abominably in the nostrils. Such
people as I passed looked apathetic, listless, hungry. Any fears I might have entertained about
being recognised were soon set at rest. The way-
farers eyed me suspiciously, furtively, slunk past
with a sidelong glance of the eye, and as soon as
they were safely behind me scurried rapidly away.
They were afraid, afraid of the nameless terror
which stalked the streets of what once had been

among the fairest of European cities. At any moment the Red Terror might pounce upon them and bear them away to the sound of their muffled screams. No one could tell in what dark doorway it lurked, in what foul alley it lay waiting, this dread monster which sated its sadistic lust upon the lives of men. Men had been alive and flourishing yesterday—as much, that is, as men in Russia could be said to flourish—and the morning dawned, and where were they? The silent dungeons of No. 2 Gorohovaya could tell a story which a man might hear and never sleep again, a story of nameless horror and revolting torture and ghastly death, a story the like of which has never been told. I for one hope it never will be told in its entirety. Who *could* tell the whole truth about Russia?

As I have said before, the Bolshevists were in a very small minority. But the population was cowed by that secret terror. It seemed to have in it an element of the supernatural. The vengeance of the Tcheka was so swift, so silent, so sure. You could trust nobody. The brother born from the same womb as you, the wife of your bosom, the woman of your heart might be in league against you. Truly the abomination of desolation is sitting where it ought not, and the forces of anti-Christ are abroad in Russia to-day.

Some few years after the events I am at present narrating, a friend of mine, whom I will call D., escaped from Russia and arrived in London destitute, but happy to have escaped with his life. Night after night in his English sanctuary he would awaken screaming in mortal terror that the forces of the Tcheka were upon him. He could never get that fear out of his mind, even by the banks of the Thames. He feared to be left alone. He was uneasy and suspicious in the company of his friends. He was in mortal terror in a crowd. Ultimately, impossible seeming though it is, he went back to Russia. His wife had been killed there, shot down by the Bolshevists while she was trying to escape. Then he heard that she was still alive. Even in London the secret visitors came for him. They were friends, of course, and anti-Bolsheviks. They told him that his wife was in prison, but that the agents of the White Russians in Moscow could secure her release, but it was imperative that he should go to Moscow himself. A forged passport had been prepared for him. All was ready. So D. went to Russia, and was never heard of again.

Now shortly after I arrived in Petrograd I knew that I was being followed. At first it was but a suspicion. A feeling of uneasiness came over me, such a feeling as I was to experience often enough before I got out of Russia. Then my suspicion gradually grew and grew until it became a certainty. One of my usual Petrograd haunts was raided. In another a trap was laid and I escaped by inches. The Tcheka had discovered something. But what? I was uneasy. My mind went back to the sinister figure of Marchand whom I had distrusted from the first.

It was imperative, however, that I should give no inkling of my suspicion that I was being followed. I decided to take a bold step and see Orlovsky at his office. The obvious fear shown by everybody I approached in Petrograd made my task comparatively easy. Anybody who approached with any degree of confidence I suspected at once of being a Bolshevik official and in my turn I avoided him, and so arrived without accident at the Fontanka quay. Here in the old days was situated the Ministry of the Interior, and here now was the headquarters of the Tcheka-Criminel, the organisation of which I was a collaborator.

A dirty and villainous-looking porter met me at the door and scrutinised me with suspicious eye and without saying a word.

"Is Veneslav Orlovsky here?" I asked him, and handed him my passport, which described me as a collaborator of the Tcheka-Criminel. The clown pondered the passport for a full minute without saying anything. It was obvious that he could not read: equally obvious that the seal on the document impressed him. At last he stamped his foot. Two Red Guards appeared out of the darkness at the back of the hall.

"Veneslav Orlovsky," said the porter. The guards placed themselves one on each side of me. We marched. We went up the stairs and arrived at the door, which led into the apartment of the President of the Tcheka-Criminel.

I remained for some time chatting with Orlov-

sky and left him at the end of about half an
hour. As a result of our consultation we concluded
that whatever might be the fate of M. Constantine,
Comrade Relinsky was not suspected.

It was mid-day and intensely hot. Nobody was
about. The Fontanka presented a spectacle of
squalor and ruin. I passed the usual bread-queues,
hungry, listless, only not rebellious, waiting, waiting for their meagre allowance of black rye bread
with the patience which is all Russia. A car swept
along the dirty, litter-strewn road containing two
Bolshevik officials. All cars had been impounded
by the Bolshevists and were at the use of the Communist authorities. *They* did not wait in food
queues. A few pairs of eyes turned and followed
the car up the street, rebellion smouldering in them
for a brief moment. Then even the light of rebellion went out, and the eyes swung round again to
the patient contemplation of the backs in front of
them. Bolshevism was one thing. In front of them
was bread.

Accordingly Comrade Relinsky ousted Mr.
Massino, and I decided for the time being to keep
away from any place where I was known under
any other identity than that of the worthy collaborator of the Tcheka. I felt perfectly safe and
reasonably optimistic.

The blow fell quite suddenly. Berzin had already returned to Moscow to put everything in
readiness as far as he was concerned. I rang up
Grammatikoff to inform him of the slight modifi-

cation of my plans and to give him the news that
Mr. Massino had left Petrograd. It was quite in
order that Comrade Relinsky should be profes-
sionally interested in the resident alien bourgeois
merchant, Mr. Massino. There was sardonic humour in Comrade Relinsky being suspicious of
Mr. Massino. Grammatikoff answered the 'phone
himself and his voice was hoarse and unnatural. It
seemed as if he was trying to disguise it.

"It is I, Relinsky," I assured him.

"Who?" asked Grammatikoff. I repeated the
name.

And then it was that the blow fell, stunning me
with the force of its sudden impact. I seemed to
plunge suddenly into the depths of a black abyss
and then fetch up with a jerk, while the walls
whirled and danced around me.

"I have somebody with me," said Grammatikoff,
"who has brought bad news. The doctors have
operated too early and the patient's condition is
serious. Come at once if you wish to see me." I
realised with a sinking feeling that Grammatikoff's
voice was not hoarse because it was disguised. It
was hoarse with horror. What could be his meaning? Something terrible had obviously happened,
something to do with our conspiracy, something of
which he dared not speak in plain terms over the
wire.

Not a conveyance was to be had for love or
money. As I have said, all motor vehicles had been

confiscated by the Bolsheviks, and converted largely to the purposes of the Tcheka-Politique. Horses starved in Russia. They were whipped to the last ounce of strength they had in them, and when they dropped, were left where they were. Until the carcase had decomposed too far, the hungry people would cut meat from it.

I hurried as much as I dared in the direction of Grammatikoff's house. One dared not hurry too much. A man who hurries had business. A man who has business is suspect in Red Russia. However, within an hour I was in Grammatikoff's flat and listened to his tale of woe. A bitter tale too it was to hear.

"The fools have struck too early," said Grammatikoff. "Uritzky is dead, assassinated in his office this morning at eleven o'clock. At the very moment when you telephoned me the bearer of the bowstring was with me. It was Hermann, a Jew, whom I know to be a genuine sympathiser of ours. 'Monsieur Grammatikoff,' he said to me, 'you must fly at once. The reprisals will be horrible. The bourgeoisie will be shot down by the thousand, and you in particular will run an enormous risk. Fly. I will try to arrange a passport for you.'"

Hermann was right. The reprisals would be horrible, and in the midst of them our conspiracy might very easily be exposed. Some poor wretch might well try to purchase his safety by telling what he knew, and the danger to ourselves and our friends was imminent.

"It is a terrible risk our staying here," said Grammatikoff. "I am, of course, already under suspicion. If anything is discovered before anything else it will be your name and mine. Moreover the *svolotch* arrested Alexandra Petrovna two days back, and the Lord alone knows what they found on her. Besides a woman, you know, and under torture. . . . Well, it is a comfort she did not know very much."

As he spoke Grammatikoff was emptying the drawers of his desk of papers and burning them in the grate. At any moment we might hear the steps of the terrible Tcheka on the stairs.

"Where will you be to-night?" I asked.

"I shall go to my sister's. And you, Sidney Georgevitch? You will not return to No. 10?"

"Yes. Mr. Massino must return to Petrograd. There are friends of his who might be implicated, and he must warn them without any delay."

We arranged a meeting for the following day and parted.

How much had the *svolotch* discovered? How many of our friends in Petrograd were suspect? Would there be an outbreak of the Red Terror following the death of Uritzky? As yet everything was quiet. Nothing had happened. The Bolsheviks had made no move. Was it possible that Hermann had been misinformed? Perhaps things were not so bad after all. If anything had happened, the

Tcheka would surely have struck by now. It was in a somewhat happier frame of mind that I reached the Torgovaya Ulitza. Elena Michailovna let me in.

I told her to prepare herself for instant flight. Her movements in just such a situation as this had been previously arranged. Then I rang up Captain Cromie, the Naval Attaché at the British Embassy, and asked him to meet me at the café kept by Serge Sergevitch Balkoff, where we had our usual *rendezvous*. A meeting was arranged for 12 o'clock. I had only time to burn my papers. I watched the last flame gutter out, the last thin wisp of smoke curl up and vanish.

"All is quiet," whispered Balkoff and led me to the little room at the back of his café. The fingers of the little clock above the mantel pointed to the hour. I was just in time. Even as the door closed behind me, the clock gave a little burr and with a high pitched tinny note struck out the hour. Cromie was not yet there.

Queer how silent it was. This place had always been busy enough in the old days, and even now under the present *régime* did not want for custom. I recalled other occasions, when I had sat here waiting for Cromie as now I was waiting, waiting for Grammatikoff when he was to reveal to me the plan by which I was to get to Moscow months before, waiting here years, years ago for Sascha, long before the Germans had put the world in a flame, when I was young and St. Petersburg was still one of the gay cities of the world. I pictured the gay throng assembled round the little tables in the café, heard in imagination the ripple of conversation, the chink of cups. How silent the place was. I waited to hear Balkoff tiptoe across the empty outer room. Silence. Five minutes past twelve.

Not like Cromie to be unpunctual. My feelings may be imagined, as I waited there. In my mind I went again over the happenings of the last two months, my high hopes and their ignominious sequel. I had been within an ace of becoming master of Russia. I would have satisfied my superiors by bringing Russia into the line against Germany. But how much more would I have done. What is happening here is more important than any war that has ever been fought. At any price this foul obscenity which has been born in Russia must be crushed out of existence, crushed out, while yet it was small. Peace with Germany? Yes, peace with Germany, peace with anybody. There is only one enemy. Mankind must unite in a holy alliance against this midnight terror.

With a whirr and a cling the little clock on the mantel struck recalling me with a start from my flight of mental rhetoric. A quarter past twelve and Cromie not here. I dared not wait any longer. Balkoff, comrade though he was, was probably suspect. But it was imperative that I should see Cromie that day.

I decided to risk a visit to the British Embassy.

It was a dangerous move, of course, both for the Embassy and myself. But I had brought it off successfully before.

The street was clear. I stepped out. Before I went I gave a word of warning to Balkoff—to be prepared to leave Petrograd and slip across the frontier into Finland.

In the Vlademirovsky Prospect I met some men and women running. They dived into doorways, into side-streets, anywhere. There was evidently a panic. What had happened? Then suddenly the cause was revealed to me. A car shot by, crammed with Red soldiers, then another, then another. The Tcheka was out.

I quickened my pace, and was almost running, when I turned into the street where the British Embassy maintained a precarious oasis of civilisation in the midst of the waste that was Petrograd. And this is what I saw:

In front of the British Embassy was arranged a line of bodies—the dead bodies of Bolshevik soldiers. Four cars were drawn up opposite, and across the street was drawn a double cordon of Red Guards. The Embassy door had been battered off its hinges. The Embassy flag had been torn down. The Embassy had been carried by storm. That line of Red bodies told that the garrison had sold the place dearly.

Suddenly a voice addressed me by name, and I spun round to find myself looking into the face of a grinning Red soldier.

"Well, Comrade Relinsky, have you come to see our carnival?"

"I have longed to see this sight," said I sweetly. "But, behold my usual luck. I ran all the way, and I am too late. Tell me, comrade, what happened?"

The man was one I had met fairly often in my guise of Comrade Relinsky of the Tcheka-Criminel, and he proceeded with the greatest gusto to tell me what had been happening, while I was awaiting Cromie at Balkoff's.

The Tcheka were endeavouring to find one Sidney Reilly, and had actually raided the British Embassy in the hope that he would be there.

In the Embassy were some forty British subjects with Woodhouse at their head. When the raid took place Woodhouse had rushed upstairs to the upper room, where were kept all the Embassy papers, which he proceeded to destroy as fast as he could. Meanwhile, the gallant Cromie, a Browning automatic in each hand, had held the stairs against the Red horde, and had emptied both magazines into them before he had fallen, literally riddled with bullets.

.   .   .   .   .

A man commonly sleeps very well on the night following a great catastrophe. It is the waking on the morning after which is often queer and upsetting. I was awake very early on the morning of the 31st, tossing on my couch and recapitulating in my mind the terrible events of the previous day. The British mission had vanished at a blow. Cromie was dead. My English associates in Petrograd were dispersed. The Tcheka was hot upon my trail. Where the next blow would fall it was impossible to say. In Moscow there were still Lockhart and Hill. What *was* happening in Moscow? In view of what had occurred the situation there must be desperate indeed. The full weight of the terror would be felt there. Somehow or other I must get my agents out of the trap. Come what might, I must go to Moscow to-day.

I had spent the night at the house of a friend, one Serge Sergeievitch Dornoski. Even while I had been at Balkoff's café, G.'s house and No. 10 had been raided.

The long fingers of the morning slowly crept in at the window as I lay there tossing with my thoughts. What was happening in Moscow? What was happening in Moscow?

I remained under cover that morning, while Serge went out and made a reconnaissance. In the course of two hours he returned, bringing with him a copy of the official Communist journal, the *Pravda*, and the news that parties of the Tcheka were busy in every quarter of Petrograd.

"The streets will run blood," was Serge's grim comment. "Uritzky has been killed in Petrograd. Somebody has had a shot at Lenin in Moscow, and unfortunately missed him. Here it all is," and he spread out the copy of the paper before me.

My eye fell on the fatal headline of that ac-
cursed *Pravda*. There had been an attempt on
Lenin. The Tcheka were carrying out a series of
raids in Moscow. They were on the track of a
mighty English conspiracy. The name of the
Cheremeteff Pereulok caught my eye. For a moment the paper swam before my eyes, the walls
rocked and surged towards me. The window
seemed to advance and recede, advance and recede.

.   .   .   .   .

"I must go back to Moscow at once."

Grammatikoff agreed with me, while letting it
be plainly seen that he regarded my chances of
getting out of Moscow alive as small indeed. He
had no definite news from Moscow, but rumour
had it that the gutters of the city were running
with blood as a reprisal for the assassination of
Uritzky and the attempt on Lenin. Nobody was
safe there. Women and children had been shot
down. Lockhart was said to be in prison. The
chances were great that my part in the conspiracy
was known.

Grammatikoff arose and walked up and down
the room in his agony.

"It is impossible for you to go to Moscow, Sidney Georgevitch," he groaned. "It is going straight
into the lion's den. Think how you are known
there. Think what their vengeance will be now
they have found out how you have tricked them.
It is horrible to think of, horrible."

He covered his eyes with his hands, as if to blot out the terrible spectacle which his imagination presented before them.

"We know nothing definite from Moscow yet," I pointed out, "and we must have some information before we decide how to act. You know what precautions we have taken. Mademoiselle S., Dagmara and the rest are staunch, and can be relied on not to betray me. And then, when it comes to the matter of being known, I am really in infinitely greater danger in Petrograd, where hundreds of people of all classes are acquainted with me or with my appearance."

"Yes, you are right," Grammatikoff admitted resignedly. "Our friends in Moscow are staunch, as you say, but you know what fiends the Redskins are, and who can remain true under much torture?"

About forty miles to the west of Moscow on the railroad is the station of Kline, where the trains stop for ten minutes or so, while tickets and passports are examined by the Red officials. The station possesses a bookstall, where papers and communist literature are to be bought. We arranged that I should proceed by rail as far as Kline, and purchase the Moscow papers there. Only if the news they contained was sufficiently reassuring was I to proceed to Moscow. Otherwise I was to return to Petrograd and confer with Grammatikoff again.

It was at Grammatikoff's sister's flat that this

conversation took place. Grammatikoff told me with a smile how when his own flat had been ransacked the previous night, the Tcheka agents had failed to notice the private telephone wire, and had only broken down the line which was registered in the telephone book. As a result he had been able to speak to his secretary this morning, giving her final orders and learning exactly what had happened during the Tcheka raid.

His conclusion was that the Tcheka could have found nothing incriminating.

"Not that they need to," he admitted with a shrug. "Petrograd is an unhealthy place these days, Sidney Georgevitch. Once a man gets the infection he dies very quickly. I must move out in a few days for reasons of health. But I will stay here a little. If you return from Kline telephone me at Dornoski's. I must get my sister away from Petrograd, that is certain."

Yes, there would be plenty of people striving to get out of Petrograd during the next few days. With the new outburst of the terror, more *émigrés* would be slipping down to the frontier, where the Finns and the Red patrols eyed each other across the narrow river. Across that river the helping hands of the Finns would be stretched out to drag the poor refugees to safety, but the Bolshevik Guards would be alert. What proportion of the fugitives would get safely over, I wondered, and what harvest of carnage would the Red soldiers reap before this fatal week was over. In imagination I saw tenderly nurtured women and brave men haled back to the grim dungeons of No. 2 Gorohovaya, when safety was already within their sight, I saw torturings and shootings and carnage, I heard the shrieks of the tormented and the groans of the dying, and the fingers of the Bolshevist's Chinese hirelings dripping blood.

It would not be easy for anyone to get out of Petrograd. The forces of the Tcheka would be at every station scrutinising the passengers as they arrived. No place could be more dangerous. However it would be easier for me, travelling to Moscow. No one would fly *to* Moscow from the Terror.

I shook hands with Grammatikoff, and slipped down into the street.

CHAPTER THREE

The teeth of the man next to me were chattering. Every time anybody looked at him he seemed to meditate instant flight. A woman near was praying under her breath. But for the most part the crowd in which we were wedged was silent and cowed. We were pressing up to the barrier of the platform from which the train departed for Moscow. In front of us at the gate was a small group of Red Guards and officials examining passports. They were making a good job of it. One by one the crowd filtered through the barrier and joined the mass of humanity on the platform.

At last I came up level with the barrier. It was a nervous moment. My pass had been signed and sealed by an official of whom I had no news since last seeing him. For all I knew his part in the conspiracy had already been discovered, or he had slipped away from his post while yet there was time. The chances that he had been discovered were certainly big.

I had already arranged my plan of campaign and was ready for all eventualities. My right hand was on the butt of my revolver. If I was to be taken I would not be the only victim. With my left hand I thrust my passport into the soldier's face, at the same time favouring him with my most malevolent stare. It was the Tcheka stare, boring him through and through. "Ah, my fine friend," it said, "in these days even a comrade might be in the pay of the cursed English, and I am not sure that I do not suspect you yourself."

Such was the message my look was meant to convey, and so did the fellow interpret it. Innocent or guilty, it was no pleasure for a Red soldier to be suspect by the Tcheka. The Tcheka had an uncanny way of proving a man's guilt.

"Collaborator of the Tcheka," said the soldier, pushing back the document to me with hardly a glance at it. "Pass, comrade."

I was on the platform and in a minute had mixed with the crowd. A compact, seething mass of humanity was pressing, swaying, forcing its way into the carriages. Others came up and burrowed their way through. The squeeze was terrific. Some of the more athletic found a place on the roof. Bolshevik Russia always travels so. For my part, in my position of a collaborator of the Tcheka-Criminel, and officer of the Extraordinary Commission, I was justified in travelling first class. Third is for the *canaille*. Comrades travel first. But I did not choose to assert my authority too strongly. I put my head down, and burrowed and wriggled my path through the swarm into one of the third-class cars, and landed bruised and breathless on the dirty floor. The carriage stank abominably and it was packed to suffocation point. Nobody spoke a word. The only sound was that of the breathing

of my travelling companions. It was quite dark.
The windows were blotted out by surplus members
of this human freight. It was insufferably hot. Outside the Black Hole of Calcutta or the hold of a
slave ship, the world can have seen few things to
compare with the interior of a Soviet train.

At last we pulled up at Kline. A number of people got out, myself among them. I walked over to
the book-stall and bought copies of the Moscow
papers. There was ten minutes to wait, and I had
ample leisure to find out exactly what was happening in Moscow. The news was not reassuring.
Through the instrumentality of Réné Marchand a
great anti-Bolshevist plot, emanating from the
Allied legations in general and the British in particular, had been discovered. The complicity of
Lockhart had been proved. Friede had been arrested and he and his sister were prisoners, the
Mlles. S. were prisoners. Berzin had made some
astounding revelations.

The game was up, and, according to my arrangement with Grammatikoff, my course was an immediate return to Petrograd. But my responsibility was too great. Through me my friends were
involved in the greatest risk, Lockhart was a prisoner, Hill, the gallant and trusty Hill, was—the
Lord knew where. And now my Russian agents
were leaderless in the midst of a city of terror. The
vengeance of the Tcheka was a ghastly thing. If I
left my friends in their present terrible plight and
slipped back to Petrograd and Finland, how could

I ever look the world in the face again? Besides something might yet be done. I might assist in the escape of some of those, who were gravely committed and as yet had avoided capture. At the worst I might offer up myself as the sole author and instigator of the plot and hostage for my friends. The whole of my scheme had collapsed, and at the moment I felt that I had nothing left to live for, and might just as well die as Cromie had done.

It took me barely a minute to decide upon proceeding to Moscow. It was pretty obvious in the present condition of affairs that I could not travel by the train and run the gauntlet of the Red inquisition at the station. And at that very moment I noticed a Red soldier and a Commissary making their way down the platform and examining the papers of the people crowded thereon. The man was only a few paces from me. There was not a moment to be lost. I edged my way back to the train, and, seizing a favourable moment, dropped on to the line and dived under the car. Of course, many people in the crowd saw me, but I did not mind that. For passengers to hide under a train while the inspection of papers is in progress is not an unusual thing in Red Russia.

As a matter of fact on this occasion I found quite a little colony of fugitives already huddled beneath the train, and my course was seriously impeded as I crawled down the track towards the rear. About fifty yards from the track I noticed a small group of trees and in them I made up my mind to take cover. Slowly I raised myself until my eye was on a level with the platform. The Commissary was busy with a poor wretch, who had fallen on his knees before him, crying and protesting; the Red soldier was fingering his bayonet suggestively. Now for it. Bending low I raced from the railway track to the friendly cover of the trees, where I threw myself on the ground on my face. As soon as I had recovered my breath sufficiently I drew myself up and reconnoitred the station. The train was just drawing out. Nobody seemed to have noticed anything.

I did not waste any time. I walked into Kline and found a peasant, who had a horse and carriage with which he was prepared to drive me to the next village in the direction of Moscow. It was about half past eight in the morning, when I left Kline, and using relays of horses from village to village I was in the outskirts of Moscow the same night. The night was dark, for which I was unfeignedly thankful. I rewarded my charioteer handsomely and watched him drive away, then walked briskly down the road into the city of the Terror.

Nobody was about. I had not the least idea where to go. The Cheremeteff Pereulok was barred to me, and it was impossible to say in what other of my accustomed haunts the blow would next fall. I was naturally extremely tired after the tedious day's journey, and wanted rest confoundedly, but I dared not visit any of my friends, until after I had made a preliminary reconnaissance. The English, of whom a few had still been living in Moscow, would all be prisoners or fugitives at the Consulate.

At last I decided to billet myself upon a White Russian, whose name and address I knew, but who personally was quite unacquainted with me. He was to have been one of Judenitch's provisional army, but otherwise was not deeply compromised, and accordingly might well have escaped suspicion. He was some sort of distant relation of Dagmara, who had reported well of him, and accordingly I was not so diffident as I might otherwise have been in trusting myself to his mercy.

Everything was silent as I slipped up the untidy litter strewn stairs of the house, and rattled at his door. People do not sleep soundly in Russia. I had but a minute to wait before steps shuffled up to the door, which was opened about half an inch, and a woman's voice, hoarse with agitation, asked,

"Who is there?"

"A friend of Dagmara K," I answered in a whisper.

"We don't know any Dagmara K," came the voice in a groan.

"I think you do," said I, completely reassured by her manner. "Do not be afraid, I am an officer and a fugitive. I want shelter. Let me in."

Immediately came the rattling of a chain, and the door was opened just wide enough to admit me.

I slipped in and the door was closed and bolted behind me. I turned round and struck a match and beheld an old lady, fully dressed, white and trembling with fear.

"Where is Ivan Stefanitch?" I asked her. "Is he in?"

"Oh, sir, we know nothing about refugees," said the old dame. "We are harmless people and know nothing of politics."

"Then I am sure you will not betray me," I said, "I am a refugee from the Soviet, and would be grateful for shelter for the night."

"What name shall I call you?" asked the lady.

"Michael Markovitch is my name," I told her. "I was an officer in the Tsar's army, and I am wanted by the Redskins for some reason best known to themselves."

"Then you are welcome to what poor shelter I can give you, Michael Markovitch," said my hostess now quite reassured, "and the good God knows it is poor enough in these days. Will you eat? We have bread, but little else, I fear."

"Thank you, at the present moment all I want is sleep."

"Come this way," said the old lady, and led me into a barely furnished room at the back. "The furniture has been taken by the house committee. It is the best I can do."

There was a mattress in the corner. I had not slept a minute for thirty-six hours. Mumbling my thanks, I threw myself down and was asleep at once. I seemed to hear the door close and a key turn in the lock, but it might have been a dream.

Somebody had flashed a torch in my face. And afterwards I had a sort of consciousness that I had heard the door close. My first move was for my revolver, and I sighed with relief as my hand encountered the butt of that trusty weapon. Then cursing myself for my casualness I groped across to the door, and put my back firmly against it before striking a match. Nobody was there.

I dragged the mattress across the floor and put it against the door. A short reconnaissance showed me that I had a good retreat through the window and a comparatively easy descent. I closed the shutter and fastened it firmly on the inside. I had been sleeping in my boots and my feet were hurting consumedly. I dared not undress, however, and having satisfied myself that the room was secure I lay down again and fell asleep.

I was awakened by a knocking at the door. I sat bolt upright, listening intently. It was broad daylight.

"Are you awake, Michael Markovitch?" whispered a familiar voice. "It is I, Dagmara K.," and in a moment the door was opened and there was Dagmara with the old lady, who had admitted me on the previous evening, and a gentleman, whom Dagmara introduced as her cousin, Boris Sergeievitch.

My hostess prepared the samovar and set some bread before us, and while we made breakfast asked whether I had been disturbed in the previous night. It appeared that Dagmara had taken refuge with her, and was actually asleep in the house at the time of my arrival. Vera Petrovna— the old lady—had at once awakened Dagmara and sent her to my room to identify me.

"And of course I would know you anywhere, Michael Markovitch," said Dagmara, and beneath her air of archness she stressed my assumed name.

Dagmara gave me an address in the Tverskoi Boulevard where I was to meet her. Shortly afterwards she left the house, and allowing her to get a little way ahead I followed.

"You are running a great risk, M. Constantine," she told me when I had rejoined her. "Vera Petrovna is closely connected with Mme. Kaplan, who made the attempt on Lenin. She might be arrested at any moment. She is all ready to fly, but at present knows not how."

So had I begun my excursion in Moscow by putting my head right in the noose.

In the meantime it will be as well if I give some account of what had actually happened in Moscow during my absence.

After the assassination of Uritzky at Petrograd and the attempt on Lenin at Moscow, Moscow was divided into a number of small sections for the purpose of the Tcheka inquisition. To each section was assigned a detachment of Tcheka agents, and every house in turn was ransacked from top to bottom. Among the other places the flat in the

Cheremeteff Pereulok was visited. Dagmara and the two sisters S. were together when the raid took place, and in a drawer of the bureau were over two million roubles in 1,000 rouble notes. When the agents of the Tcheka thundered on the door, demanding admission, Dagmara had picked up a bundle of notes and thrust them between her legs, and there had kept them during the whole period of the search. The Tcheka agents, who were tiring of their task, conducted a very superficial examination, left the apartment and descended the staircase. As they came down they met a girl coming up with a portfolio under her arm.

"Where are you going?"

"To visit Mlle. S."

"Show us that portfolio."

It was the end. The girl was Mlle. Friede, who, as I have mentioned before, used to bring copies of the Bolshevik secret documents from her brother to my headquarters in the Cheremeteff Pereulok. Mlle. Friede was arrested at once. The agents of the Tcheka returned to Mlle. S.'s apartment. During their absence safety measures had been taken. The money had been hidden securely. None the less the two sisters were arrested. Colonel Friede was arrested. Berzin was arrested. By an extraordinary stroke of fortune Dagmara was allowed to go free. Such was the remarkable story which Dagmara told me that day in the house in the Tverskoi Boulevard, almost opposite to the "Tramble" Café, where I had met Berzin so many times. And so had the most promising plot ever concocted against the Bolsheviks been broken down by the folly of Mlle. Friede. As absolutely every motor car in Russia had been confiscated by the Bolsheviks, it was understood, not only among my agents, but in general, never to enter a house before which stood a motor car. It was a sure sign that the Tcheka was there. But poor Mlle. Friede had become so used to danger in the two months, during which she had acted as my agent, that she had neglected a most simple and elementary precaution. Our plot had ended in a fiasco.

My meeting with Dagmara was invaluable. I was enabled to gather up the broken threads of my organisation in Moscow. A price was on my head. I was an outlaw. I was to be shot at sight by anyone who identified me. My real identity was known. My *noms de guerre*, Constantine and Massino, were known. Everything was uncovered. Now that I was in the city of the Terror, my chances of getting out again were, I had to admit, very small.

In the meantime I must lie low and watch points. Spasmodic raids were taking place at every hour in Moscow. People were being arrested by the thousand. Usually there was not a particle of evidence against them. But they were bourgeoisie. That was enough.

Chapter Four

Never in my life have I been so
talked about. My name was in everybody's mouth.
My description was pasted up all over Moscow. I
cropped up in every conversation—myself and
Bruce Lockhart. Lockhart, as I have previously
shown, was absolutely ignorant of my conspiracy,
but the Bolsheviks were determined to drag the
Allied missions into it. And Bruce Lockhart was
now a prisoner, and it was up to me, if his life
were really in danger, to surrender myself in his
place. All Moscow had gone rabid. The discovery
of my conspiracy had been the spark to ignite the
magazine.

All my names and aliases were known. They
were published in the official Bolshevist journal
together with the proclamation of my outlawry.
They were all there—Relinsky, Constantine, Massino and the rest. My arch enemies had identified
me at last under my various disguises with Sidney
George Reilly of the British service.

But of my whereabouts nothing was known.
Some said that I was in hiding in Petrograd, some
that I was in Finland, some that I had returned to
England. Some even went so far as to suggest that
I was actually in Moscow itself—there in the very
lions' den. I was the most talked of man in the

place. I cannot say that I entirely appreciated the unsought publicity.

"They say he has actually been seen in Moscow," said Nicholas Nicholaivitch to me. Nicholas had been an officer in the old Imperial Army, and knew me as Serge Dmitrievitch. Fugitives were not asked more than their first name and patronymic in the days of the terror. "They say this Reilly has actually been seen in Moscow. Our friends of the Tcheka are having another little series of raids for him, and, believe me, if he is here, I pity him. They are very thorough, the Tcheka. Not even a mouse could escape them. The *svolotch* wiped out thirty whole families last night, thirty, my word of honour. Up against the wall, and pop, pop, pop, man, woman and child."

"And if this Reilly is in Moscow?" I suggested.

"Oh they will find him," said Nicholas Nicholaivitch. "Nothing escapes them in the end. You don't know where and when their hand is coming to grab you. You do not know *who* are your enemies these days. Oh yes, they will find him."

"And then?"

"And then——" Nicholas Nicholaivitch put his great fingers round his throat and made an unpleasant clicking noise. He laughed—the monster actually laughed. It was curious how dispassionately, not to say good humouredly the anti-revolutionaries would discuss my probable fate.

"But seriously, Serge Dmitrievitch," said

Nicholas' wife, "when do you think the Allies will come? They have been coming—oh so long. Will they really come? One hears rumours. Now they are here, now there, now they are within a day's march of Vologda, now they have taken Cronstadt. Pray God they will be in time."

It was a prayer that was going up to the Father of Mercies in many parts of Moscow at that time. The Allies had been expected so long, there were so many rumours, so many hopes doomed to frustration. Would they really come? The populace as a whole was sure of it. Russia might yet be saved. But time passed and the Allies did not come. A terrible thing had arisen in Russia, which, if it were not checked, would spread like a slime over the whole world, foul, reeking, obscure. All the civilisation which had taken so many thousands of years to build would be slowly engulfed in that filthy flood, and the last note of joy would die in the mouth of the world.

I did not spend two nights in the same place or under the same name. Now I was a Greek merchant, whose flat had been seized by a workman's family, now I was a Tsarist officer, seeking escape from Moscow, now I was a Russian merchant, trying to avoid the military service which the Bolsheviks had made compulsory.

I had my introduction to all these good people, who gave me shelter during my precarious stay in Moscow. I know the names and addresses of many of the conspirators, with whom I was not personally acquainted. I knew also who were the other members of their "Five." For the rest the Bolsheviks were of the very greatest assistance to me. They were so conceited over the discovery of the conspiracy that, from day to day, they published the fullest reports of the progress they were making. In consequence I knew who had been arrested, who was likely to be under suspicion, where I could go without fear of disturbance.

As soon as it grew dark I would creep round to one of the addresses. Making sure that the coast was clear, I would slip in and ring at the door. Then would follow the usual ritual. The door would be poked slightly ajar and a quavering, frightened voice would ask who was there. The formula was always the same.

"Serge Ivanitch"—or whoever it was—"Serge Ivanitch told me you would allow me to sleep here to-night." Then I would give my assumed name and some specious reason for having no abode of my own.

It was in this way that I billeted myself on the cheerful Nicholas Nicholaivitch. Every night it was somewhere else. Rarely, I fear, was I a welcome guest. My coming would reduce my host—or hostess-to-be, to a pitch of the most extreme terror. Their whole attitude would be crying out more eloquently than words, "Oh for God's sake leave me alone, for God's sake leave me alone." I would see their lips twitch and their eyes go blank with nameless terror, and the whole bodies would quiver and shake as if in an ague, but I was never refused.

Many people were finding shelter like that in Moscow during those days. My brave friend and coadjutor, Captain Hill, was in hiding too, moving from place to place like myself, and assuming a similar variety of disguises. We would meet and confer together for a short time during the day. The work which had brought me to Moscow went on.

The last feeble spark of normal life, which had flickered during the past few months in Moscow, had now guttered out. Everywhere there was an increasing dearth of all the necessities of life. Everything spoke of stagnation. The only people one saw in the dirty, litter-strewn streets were the bread-queues, listlessly waiting to have filtered out to them from the dirty hands of the food controllers their meagre supply of dirty bread against their food tickets. There was never enough to go round. All day the wretched, starving people stood there. They arrived at an unearthly hour in the morning to be in time. If they were lucky they received their wretched dole and carried it hastily away. Hunger had tempted them into the streets again. Every now and then a raid would take place. The Tcheka cars would drive up, and the Red soldiers dismount with their prodigiously long rifles and bayonets. Then the Commissar—the People's Commissar as he was ironically called—

would proceed down the queue examining passports.

Now and then the street would be blocked by
Red soldiers at each end, and all the people who
were in it were stopped and interrogated. Arrests
were frequent. Whether the victims were shot,
tortured or confined in the terrible Butyrsky, who
knows? People might wonder for the rest of their
lives which had happened to their friends. Wives
would leave their husbands in the morning to
stand in the queues and never return. They were
swallowed in the stygian night. Better by far to
know that they had been killed and were out of it,
out of it all. Better by far to know that they were
dead than confined in the terrible Butyrsky, that
haunt of slaughter, sadism and nameless horrors.

The Tcheka raids were conducted with a degree
of callousness and brutality which to a civilised
mind is inconceivable. On one occasion, when the
inhabitants of one apartment failed to remove the
chain from the door through the extremity of terror, a Red soldier threw a bomb through the opening. In another place they had no response to their
knockings. Their victim this time was an old lady,
confined to her bed through a stroke, which had
resulted from the murder of her husband before
her eyes during the massacres of the previous year.
Nobody else was in the flat and one of the Red
soldiers, impatient at the delay, threw a grenade
at the door. The bomb exploded, killing or wound-
ing five soldiers. The soldiers returned that night

and butchered the old lady in her bed as a "reprisal" for the damage.

The evacuation of my agents from Moscow was
now proceeding apace. Some managed to obtain
their passage to Petrograd, some got to Vologda.

I was exceedingly perturbed by the position of
Mlle. S. I had an agent at work, who was prepared
to pay a considerable sum to secure her release.
Through this man I was introduced to a certain
M., the friend of an Investigator of the Tcheka.

I represented myself as a relation of Mlle. S.,
and asked M. how much it would cost to induce his
friend the Investigator to turn the evidence in her
favour. M. thought the matter might be done for
50,000 roubles.

"Of course we must remember," said M., "that
the case of your cousin—did you say that she was
your cousin?—is peculiar. The arrest has attracted
a lot of attention. The evidence against her is almost conclusive. To be sure they will keep her
alive, until they have got all the information they
can from her, and that of course gives us a certain
amount of time in which to act. But the point is
that the case against her is strong. No Investigator
can let her off and go untouched. Our man will
have to be well covered and he will have to flee
himself. It can be done, but it will be expensive.
Still, as Mlle. S. is your cousin—you did say she
was your cousin, didn't you?"

I was suspicious of this M. He had a sidelong
glance and a way of pushing questions at one,

which made me nervous. He would drop an apparently casual remark, and then he would shoot a keen glance at me to see what effect it had upon me.

"By the way," said M., "have you heard that Sidney Reilly is in Moscow?" and he gave me one of his sharp glances.

"I am not interested in Sidney Reilly," I said with no very strict regard to the truth. "About Mlle. S.?"

"Ah yes, about Mlle. S.," said M. "It is, I have said, likely to be expensive. Moreover you have to take into consideration the lady's weak state of health. I understand that she was under cross-examination for eight hours yesterday, and of course during examination the prisoner is not allowed to eat or sit down. In the circumstances it would be as well for me to arrange for some conveyance to take Mlle. S. from the Butyrsky."

Our negotiations were never completed. I found that M. had been lying to me. All that I know is that he made out of the transaction some 10,000 roubles, which I had paid him in advance.

This business had a sequel, which caused me considerable anxiety. One of my agents reported to me that our friend M. had approached him with a scheme which he had worked out for the escape of Sidney Reilly from Moscow. A forged passport was to be secured, railway officials were to be bribed and a passage opened for the hunted man to the Finnish frontier.

It became obvious that M. was a *provocateur*.

It also became obvious that the Bolsheviks, to say the least, very strongly suspected my presence in Moscow. The net was slowly being drawn round me, but by now my work in Moscow was approaching completion.

Had M. recognised me? Were the pursuers really close upon my trail? M. said that they were. When he approached my agent, he described me as already surrounded, and his plan for my escape was proportionately expensive. It could not be done, he said, under 100,000 roubles. Then one morning an attack was made on the French and American Consulates. But Poole, Grenard and the others had been warned in time, and had taken hurried refuge in the Norwegian Embassy. The Norwegian Embassy was promptly closely invested by the Red Agents, and the French and American consuls were close prisoners there for more than a week. Kalamatiano endeavoured to make good his escape to the same port of refuge. He was caught in the attempt and hauled before the Revolutionary Tribunal. As a result of documents found on him, a further large number of arrests were made.

But the British Government had a card up its sleeve. In its turn it had arrested in British territory Zinoviev and a number of other Russian communists. With them in its hand it began to bargain for the release of the British subjects who were in the trap in Moscow. But of course neither I nor my Russian agents could look for relief from this quarter.

I was very uneasy about my meeting with M. On top of this one of my agents was seized shortly after leaving me, was hauled up before the Extraordinary Commission and escaped by a miracle. How he managed to bluff his captors will puzzle me to my dying day. The Tcheka never erred on the side of leniency towards the prisoner. In fact many genuine and ardent Communists became their victims.

As if to add to my difficulties came the seizure of Kalamatiano and the wholesale arrests which followed it.

At this time I was quite without cover. I dared reveal myself to no one. I shrank from meeting people of any sort and for a few nights took shelter in an empty room, where I existed without food or cigarettes. It was the latter I missed chiefly.

At last came relief. One of the conspirators managed to get to me with food, clothes and cigarettes, and the news moreover that he had arranged for me to sleep that night at the home of some friends. And that night I slept in a warm bed for the first time for many days.

But my security was not to last. Early on the following morning my ear caught the dreaded noise of one of the large motor cars, which the Tcheka used in their raids. The mere sound of these cars would create a panic whenever it was heard.

Our house was being raided. Nearer and nearer came the secret police. Doors were flung open.

Muffled screams could be heard. The tramp of feet sounded in the next room. It was now or never. The fate of myself and my hosts was in the balance. I put on my coat and walked out. At the gate a Red Guard was standing puffing viciously at a cigarette.

I strolled slowly over towards him, pulling out a cigarette of my own.

"Give me a fire, comrade."

He handed me his cigarette, from which I lit my own. I thanked him and strolled on into the street.

It was a narrow escape and again I had nowhere to go. I decided to try to get into one of the fashionable *maisons de pesse*. These places were about the only houses which were rarely searched. I knew the woman who kept this place and of course I took a great risk as she knew who I was. But it is very often just these fallen women who are greater patriots than their more respectable sisters. They took me in at once and I stayed in a room belonging to one of the prostitutes. They made me most comfortable and the girl herself went with a message to my associates to inform them of my new hiding-place. It must be understood that anybody known to have given me shelter or food would have been instantly condemned to death. But these women did not care, and when I finally left them they refused every payment I offered them.

CHAPTER FIVE

My work in Moscow was at an end. Nearly all of my Russian agents had already left the city; the few who remained were not in immediate danger. I entertained no further fears for Capt. Hill's safety. The day before we had decided that the best plan was for him to come out of his concealment and unobtrusively to rejoin the British Mission which now, during Lockhart's imprisonment, was in charge of Capt. Hicks. The latter acquiesced and Hill was included in the list of Britishers for whose evacuation negotiations were in progress with the People's Commissaries.

It now remained for me only to arrange for my trip to Petrograd. During several days one of my agents had been investigating the possibilities of my making this trip in safety by railway. His reports were not encouraging. All the railway stations were watched, no passengers were permitted to buy tickets without presenting their identification papers, a special control had been installed at the entrance to the train platforms and all passengers had to submit to a searching examination at two points en route, at Tver and at Luga. The chances of my slipping successfully through this chain of controls seemed very slim. I had nearly decided to attempt the northern round-about route *via* Vologda, intending to get on the train at a station which I could have reached on foot some distance out of Moscow, when one of my agents, Mme. D., suggested that she might be able to obtain for me a ticket to Petrograd at the agency of the International Sleeping Car Co.

Such a ticket procured in advance meant three immense advantages: (1) it obviated my exposing myself to the danger of recognition while in a queue before the ticket office at the station, (2) it spared me the necessity of identifying myself when buying the ticket, and (3) as sleeping cars were almost exclusively used by the Commissars and by privileged persons, there was the likelihood of the examination of holders of sleeping car tickets being much less rigorous.

Mme. D. had a friend at the sleeping car agency and, being a very attractive and clever woman, she relied upon her natural advantages to persuade him to issue a ticket without his asking too many embarrassing questions. The ticket was to be for an aged relative, who was too feeble to come to the agency in person.

Mme. D. had no success at her first call at the agency, all tickets had been sold out for the 11th, and she was asked to return the next day. She did, and it seemed that she would not fare any better as again all the tickets had been sold out. She was already on the point of leaving, when her ticket-selling friend called her back and told her that a telephone message had just come through from the

German Embassy cancelling one of the two berths which had been engaged for a couple of attachés going to Petrograd. Like a hawk, Mme. D. pounced upon this extraordinary chance and extracted from her friend the precious ticket for her feeble relative, Georg Bergmann.

This latest of my aliases was part and parcel of a rather doubtful passport which Capt. Hill had procured some time ago and which, in an emergency, he intended to use himself. As he was now on the point of re-assuming his identity, he generously made me a present of the document. It had been issued, or pretended to have been so, under the old *régime*, to a certain Georg Bergmann, merchant, born in Riga in the 'eighties, i.e. at least ten years after I had made my entrance into this world. This chronological discrepancy, however, was fully compensated by two most excellent features of this identifying document: it had no photograph attached to it, and the description of Herr Bergmann was so vague that, at a pinch and with the expenditure of some force of argumentation, I could claim it as my own. Besides, I had been compelled to destroy all other identifying documents, so that for the time the Bergmann passport was my only documentary standby. It was a case of "Hobson's choice" and so I became Herr Georg Bergmann. As will be seen later, I had never any reason to regret it.

My greatest difficulty had been brilliantly solved by the resourcefulness of Mme. D. I not only had a ticket for Petrograd, but I also had the incredible piece of luck of being able to travel in a compartment engaged by the German Embassy! The rest would be easy!

My last hours in Moscow I spent in the office of the Armenian merchant, who, believing me to be a Russian officer seeking to avoid mobilisation by the Bolsheviks, had given me shelter the night before. Capt. Hill came to say good-bye to me and brought me as a present a pair of his own hairbrushes which I had frequently praised for the hardness of their bristles. This simple kindness touched me greatly.

Capt. Hill gave me the news that Lockhart's release was expected shortly and that the negotiations for the evacuation of the members of the British Mission were proceeding hopefully. This news greatly relieved my mind as to my personal responsibility for the trouble and discomfort which the members of the Mission had experienced during the last fortnight. I gave Capt. Hill detailed instructions as regards the official report he was to make about our activities in the event of my failing to reach London and also about some of my private affairs. Throughout this interview I felt that Capt. Hill had very little faith in the success of my escape and that he did not expect to see me alive again. On this rather pessimistic note we parted. Nearly two—for me very eventful—months passed before we met again in the Savoy Hotel in London.

My train was leaving at 8.30 p.m. I had decided

that my best chance of slipping into the train unobserved was as close as possible to the time of its
departure. It was important to avoid as far as lay
in my power the examination of my sole document,
the Bergmann passport. In this I again was fa-
voured by chance. Just as I was ready to start a
terrific shower began to deluge the city. Like once
before, in Petrograd, I took advantage of this truly
heaven-sent opportunity.

The station was crowded with people who were
trying to take refuge from the rain and the station
guards had their hands full in keeping back the
crowds. I managed to squeeze through into the
station, and almost immediately the first bell was
sounded for the departure of the Petrograd train.
The entrance to the platform was guarded by a
railway official and a soldier, around whom was
surging a small crowd of passengers whose papers
and tickets were being examined. I edged close to
the entrance on the left where the official was
posted. There was a violent altercation between
an old lady and the soldier over some irregularity
in her papers. The soldier appealed to the railway
official who eagerly joined in the fray. The second
bell went and the crowd of passengers surged forward. "Now or never!" I said to myself, and with
one strong push I squeezed through and found
myself on the other side of the guarded line. Not
daring to look back, and with no apparent hurry,
although with considerable inner trepidation, I
walked to the sleeping car.

The conductor inspected my ticket and showed me to the compartment. Knowing that my fellow passenger would be German, I entered the compartment with a very hearty "Guten Abend." A dark, slightly built, rather bookish looking man, with eyeglasses and dressed in a cut-away morning coat, jumped up from his seat, bowed from the waist a couple of times and echoed "Guten Abend! Guten Abend!" I bowed and again assured him that the evening was good. It certainly was—so far!

"So, Sie sprechen Deutsch; na, das ist ja wunderschön!" were his next words.

I assured him that I did. He seemed delighted with this information, and an atmosphere of goodwill was immediately established.

Just then the third bell clanged and the train began to move out of the station. I heaved a sigh of relief: I was out of Moscow!

Very soon my fellow traveller confided to me that he had been only a few days in Moscow; that he had been invalided from the Army and sent out by a group of German newspapers and attached to the German Embassy as an unofficial observer on economic conditions in Russia; and that, not knowing a word of Russian (I was delighted to hear this!) he found it awfully hard to make head or tail of the situation.

"Das ist ja hier ein wahres Irrenhaus," he said, and I had to compliment him on his rapidly acquired perspicacity.

I had to give confidence for confidence, and I told him that I was a native of the Baltic Provinces and an art dealer; that I had come to Moscow to buy antiques, but that I had experienced considerable annoyance from the Bolshevik authorities and was now returning to Riga in order to be once more "unter uns Deutsche" and away from these wild Russians!

We were now practically countrymen, and in the succeeding hours our friendship grew fast.

At first our conversation was all about art. I had been a collector all my life and I had no difficulty in entertaining my newly-found friend on this subject. Later we turned to politics. He was tremendously eager to gather information on Russian conditions and I did my best to oblige him. With typical German thoroughness he proceeded to make copious notes of my information with the object of incorporating them, as he said, in his first report to Berlin. Whenever I gave him what he considered to be a particularly interesting item, he would chuckle with delight and anticipation of his superiors' praise, and would exclaim: "Aber das ist ja köstlich . . . aber das ist ja hoch interessant; das *muss* ich aufschreiben."

How much more delightful, if only my German friend had known it, was to me the idea that I, a British Intelligence officer, was supplying him with material for his official report!

We had been travelling for a couple of hours; I had hardly eaten anything that day and I had become very hungry. I knew that Mme. D. had packed into my small battered suitcase a paper parcel containing some food. I got the parcel and suggested to my companion that he should share my repast. He told me that the butler at the Embassy had provided him with a large food parcel and suggested that we should pool our provisions and make a picnic of it. We ordered tea from the car attendant and proceeded to unpack our parcels. His parcel disclosed a wealth and variety of food, the sight of which made my mouth water. There was a roasted chicken, a meat pie and a profusion of cakes. For weeks I had not seen such miracles of the culinary art!

I did not know what was in my parcel, but I felt sure that it could only be very plain food, and I felt a sense of awkwardness when opening it in the presence of my epicure friend.

There it was: a piece of veal cut into slices, some black bread, some hard boiled eggs, a piece of butter, some sugar and half a Dutch cheese!

Abashed I showed my victuals to the German. Had I exhibited to him a live pup his look of amazement could not have been greater. I felt puzzled, possibly somewhat hurt.

"Sie haben ja Käse!" he almost screamed, grasping the cheese, staring at it with the utmost surprise and turning it to all sides, as if wishing to assure himself that it was really there.

"Das ist ja unglaublich; das ist ja wunderschön; das ist ja köstlich!" followed a string of other superlatives in praise of the cheese.

I was genuinely puzzled and asked my friend to explain his transports. It appeared that he had not eaten cheese since leaving the Army; that cheese could not be bought by the civilian population in Germany for love or money; that he was "leidenschaftlich (passionately)" fond of cheese and especially Dutch cheese; that he had been looking for cheese in Moscow, but in vain; and that therefore the sight of my cheese had stirred him so profoundly!

I assured him that nothing could give me greater pleasure than his acceptance of the cheese as a memento of our acquaintance.

Despite his protestations, I finally gained my point and he accepted what was left of the cheese after our meal was concluded. We made a very enjoyable repast, and I think that weight for weight I had eaten almost as much of his cakes as he of my cheese.

It was now past midnight; my companion, replete with cheese, was getting drowsy; presently he stretched himself out on his couch and went to sleep.

The feeling of elation which had possessed me throughout the evening over the initial success of my escape began to wane now, under the chilling influence of silence and darkness. My thoughts returned to the recent events in Moscow and Petrograd, and the "might have been's" crept out of all the recesses of my brain and assailed me with renewed vehemence.

If Réné Marchand had not been a traitor; if Berzin had not shown the white feather; if the Expeditionary Force had advanced quickly on Vologda; if I could have combined with Savinkoff; if, if, if . . . one after another they came upon me and stabbed me.

I thought of Cromie and his prophetic words to me in July, "If I do not leave by the beginning of August, *they* will surely get me!" And now he was dead! Had he been punctual to his appointment with me on that fateful Saturday, August 30th, he would have been alive now. Ten minutes' delay determined the difference between life and death for him. Anyway, he was out of it now. Need not trouble how to save his skin as I am doing . . . had died like a soldier—defiant and fighting. . . . Wish Lockhart had accepted my offer to come forward and take all the blame for the conspiracy on myself. . . . Would have gloried in standing up to the scum and hurling my contempt at them. . . . Death? far better than this miserable flight! . . . To what end? Duty? The Chief! Return to one's unit. . . . Report? What good have all our reports done? Will they, over there, ever understand that what is happening here is a far greater thing than the whole bally war? That to win the war and to lose here is still to lose and far more disastrously! To-day this appalling cancerous growth could still be arrested with a quick thrust of the knife; to-morrow it will be too late! the slimy octopus will throw its tentacles over the world and strangle it as it has strangled Russia! Russia—mutilated, defiled, spat upon, gory like a woman violated by a drunken rabble!

Peace, peace on any terms—and then a united front against the true enemies of mankind. . . .

. . . . .

It had grown very dark in the compartment, and it seemed as if billow upon billow of a greyish cloud was rolling in upon me and was going to engulf me. On and on the billows came, and the denser they grew the lighter I became until I seemed to lose weight and become part of the cloud. . . .

Presently a stout little peasant woman stepped out of the cloud and sat herself down beside me. On her head was a black shawl, in one hand she had a stick and in the other she carried a basket as if on her way to market.

"Ah, batiushka (little father)," she said, "what times we have come to! Bread at three roubles a pound, and even then you can't get it! The blood-suckers! the ogres! it is all their fault."

Her face was familiar to me. It was the same woman whom I had once seen put out of a tram-way car for loudly villifying some Red Guards. I now remembered her perfectly.

I tried to calm her, whispering that she may be overheard and arrested.

"Arrest me? Ha! Ha! Ha!" she shrieked with laughter. "Let them try it! I am not afraid of them! Ha! Ha! Ha! . . . Do you know who I am? I am Russia! Yes, sir, that very same! The little mother Russia! I am deathless! I will wait a little while longer and then I will kill them all, like dogs, like mangy dogs; with this stick I will beat them to death. And I have also brought my basket with me . . ."—she finished rather unexpectedly and faded into the darkness. . . .

And now a procession was coming out of the cloud; an endless stream of men, women and children. The crosses and banners were waving over them like a sea of ripe corn. At the head of the procession walked He, the Patriarch, in shimmering golden vestments, a white mitre with a white flowing veil on his head. The end of the veil was carried by a short stocky man, with black piercing eyes, a black goatee and dressed from head to foot in black leather.

I instantly recognised him as Sverdloff, the president of the Republic. I saw him draw an enormous pistol from his belt and take aim at the back of the Patriarch.

"Lord have mercy upon us! Lord have mercy upon us!" chanted the people, and the billows of greyish cloud caught up the prayer and bore it upwards. Nobody seemed to be aware of the Patriarch's danger.

Desperately I tried to rouse myself, to rush towards him, to scream. . . . I could not move a

limb, my voice would not come. . . . I was paralysed. In my agony I began to pray, inwardly, and
in frantic haste—and the miracle came to pass. I
had regained my freedom of movement, I rushed
towards the Patriarch and Sverdloff—when a
monstrously big Red Guard stepped in front of me
and cried "Halt!"

.   .   .   .   .

With a jerk I awoke. The nightmare had dispersed. The train had stopped. I peered through
the window. There was the usual bustle and noise
of a station. "Tver—Station Tver—ten minutes'
stop!" a conductor was calling. "Here is the passport control!" flashed through my mind, and with
this I was wide awake and bracing myself to meet
the coming ordeal.

A few minutes later I heard the tread of heavy
footsteps, the banging of doors and the coarse
voices so typical of the followers of the new social
order. I threw myself on my couch, pretending to
be asleep.

Presently the examination of the passengers in
the compartment next to ours was completed and
with a wrench our door was opened. A Commissar,
a Red Guard and the car attendant stood in the
door.

"Dokumenti poljaluite (Please show your documents)!" said the Commissar.

I half rose and in an aggrieved voice, mimicking

a German accent, said: "What documents? We are members of the German Embassy!"

The Commissar looked questioningly at the car attendant. "Da, da (yes, yes)," said the latter, "this compartment has been engaged by the German Embassy."

"Then why did you not say so at once?" said the Commissar, and the car attendant began to mumble excuses.

I resumed my reclining position. With that inward sigh of relief only the Lord knows!

"Vinovat (Excuse me)," said the Commissar, touching his cap, and was gone.

My companion, who had been only half awake during the foregoing scene, had now roused himself sufficiently to ask me what it was all about. I explained to him that this was the usual ticket control, and that I had told the inspector not to bother him because he was a member of the German Embassy.

"Das war sehr nett von Ihnen," he opined and went to sleep again.

After we had left Tver I called the attendant and told him that I should appreciate it greatly if he would arrange that we were not disturbed by the next control at Luga. I gave him a generous tip and he promised to do his best. To make quite sure he would paste a label, with the words, "German Embassy," on the door of our compartment.

With complete faith in the diplomatic immunity thus bestowed upon me, I laid myself down and passed into the soundest sleep I had experienced for a long time.

When I awoke, it was light and about 8 a.m. We were nearing Petrograd and with it the most critical stage in my journey.

The danger of recognition and arrest, great as it was in Moscow, was multiplied tenfold in Petrograd. I was known in Petrograd to hundreds of persons, any one of whom might happen to be in the station on my arrival; now, in the full glare of the day, I could be recognised by passengers on the train, some of whom might be Tcheka agents. Finally, persons who knew me may have been posted intentionally at the station exits.

A Russian proverb says: "Fear has big eyes." Certainly, the eyes of my fear were very large that morning.

Taught by the experience of the night, I knew that my safety lay in sticking as closely as possible to my companion.

I enquired of him what his intentions were on arriving in Petrograd. He told me that he was going to the German Consulate-General and that he expected to be met at the station by an automobile and by a German soldier who would take care of the Embassy's mail which he had brought from Moscow.

I heaved a sigh of relief. My difficulties had again been unexpectedly solved for me.

Hardly had the train come to a stop in the Nicolai Station, when two German soldiers, dressed in field grey uniform, rushed up to our car. I doubt whether during the entire course of the war any British officer was so glad to see German soldiers as I was at that moment.

I pointed them out to my companion, and he ordered them to take charge of the luggage. On the platform, not without some manœuvring on my part, we formed into a little procession; the two privates with the luggage in front, we two following on their heels.

I had pulled my cap deep over my eyes and was frequently raising my hand to my face as if stroking my chin. We passed through the platform control (where all the passengers were held up for inspection) without any hindrance. My carelessly muttered announcement "German Embassy" supported by the presence of the two German soldiers cleared the way for us.

A few steps more and we were at the bottom of the station stairs and in the Nicolai Square, where a car was awaiting my German friend. I had purposely already exchanged with him the usual amenities, had received once more his thanks for the cheese, had promised to look him up at the Consulate and therefore could now bid him an abbreviated good-bye.

At this early hour the square was fairly empty and, fearing that with my bag I was too evidently a new arrival and might attract the curiosity of some zealous Tcheka agent, I accepted the offer of a needy looking individual to carry my bag for me.

Together we crossed the square and dived into the maze of streets adjoining the Ligovka quarter. A quarter of an hour later I dismissed the man with a moderate tip, assured myself that I was not being followed, and made my way to the house of a friend.

I felt sure that for a few days at least I had reached a haven of much needed rest!

CHAPTER SIX

I was well satisfied with the change in my appearance. Looking in the mirror I was sure that nobody would recognise me. My beard was a really formidable affair, and gave me a most ruffianly appearance. I had allowed my hair to grow and entirely neglected the civilised practice of washing. This, in conjunction with a very shabby coat and a pair of shabbier trousers, presented a spectacle which any tramp might envy, and which the most suspicious comrade would pass unchallenged.

My intention now was to leave Russia as soon as I could. The mission on which I had been sent by the British Government had failed disastrously. There was little or no chance of picking up again the threads of my organisation in Petrograd. I had been formally condemned to death by the Bolshevik Government, the sentence to be executed whenever and wherever I was found. In short, there was little point and much danger in my remaining in Russia.

There were two ways of getting out of the country.

(1) I might take the train from the Finland station at Petrograd and cross the frontier near

Viborg. This was the favourite route of *émigrés*. The Finns were always ready to assist, but the Red patrols were correspondingly alert. However, escapes by this route were frequent. It entailed securing another passport and running the usual barrage at the railway station.

(2) There was the way over the frontier bridge at Bielo 'ostrof. This necessitated a handsome bribe to the station Commissar and to the sentry on duty at the bridge.

Fortunately I was well supplied with money. The notes at the Cheremeteff Pereulok had remained undiscovered, and, although the evacuation of my agents from Moscow had proved a costly business, I still had a considerable sum left.

Not caring about facing the inquisition at the station, I determined to follow the latter route. The panic which had followed the shooting of Uritzky had now died down. Five hundred prisoners had been executed by way of a reprisal, and the Bolsheviks had proclaimed their intention of revenging in the same fashion any further attack upon their authority. It seemed to be known that I had travelled from Moscow to Petrograd. But the Tcheka raids had ceased in the latter city and the place had resumed its normal state of stagnation.

I resolved accordingly to show myself in public and test the efficacy of my disguise. In Petrograd I had stayed with friends, moving from place to place as I had done at Moscow. This was necessary owing to the vigilance of the house-committees, particularly in the days following the discovery of the plot, in watching for unregistered lodgers. The slightest carelessness would not only lead to my discovery, but would bring the wrath of the Tcheka on to the heads of my hosts.

I was obsessed with the impression that Petrograd possessed eyes and all the eyes were focussed on me. Everybody was watching me. The man I passed just now—did he not turn round and look after me? The woman opposite, staring at me across the pavement? I was certain to be recognised and arrested. Well, I had a Colt in my pocket, and there would be a few fresh faces in Hell before I put the last bullet into my own head, rather than fall into the hands of that scum.

Gradually I grew more confident in the extent of the change in my appearance. I did not venture out in broad daylight to start with, but remained under cover until dusk. But as time went on and I still remained unrecognised, I made excursions into the more frequented streets at all hours of the day. I passed people whom I knew. I did not force myself upon their notice, however, but shuffled hurriedly by in the gait which I had assumed to suit my general appearance.

It was in the Nevsky Prospekt that I met the man who recognised me. I passed someone whose appearance was vaguely familiar to me. He seemed to know me, too, for he shot a keen and suspicious glance in my direction as he passed. Then he turned round, overtook me by about ten paces, then came back and looked at me again. I pushed ahead quickly, but before long I heard his steps tap-tapping after me again.

Then my heart missed a beat. A voice hissed over my shoulder in a hoarse whisper.

"Sidney Georgevitch!" Then as I neither turned round nor said anything he went on: "Do not be afraid. It is a friend." Thereupon he gave me an address and a number in the Kamenostrovsky Prospekt, and added—"In half an hour."

I shuffled on. Should I go? Was it a trap? No, surely if he had been an enemy he would have given the alarm there and then. Well, trap or not, I was discovered now. Might as well face it. So I went down the long Kamenostrovsky Prospekt and knocked at the door of the house indicated.

I was admitted cautiously by the man who had recognised me, and ushered into a room bare and almost denuded of furniture. My unknown ac-quaintance then swung round and peered at me narrowly.

"That beard changes you, Sidney Georgevitch," he said. "Your closest friend might not have known you."

"Perhaps that is why I have grown it," I sug-gested. "But may I ask who you are and how you came to know me?"

"I am the man who used to prevent that beard

from growing, Sidney Georgevitch," he replied. "Don't you know me yet?"

Then memory came to me. "You are the barber," I said. "You are Alexander, who used to be in Maullé's saloon, and shaved me in the old days."

Alexander seemed as pleased at the meeting as I was, and prepared the samovar in high spirits.

"Why you should have come to Russia again I do not know," he said, "when you were safely out of the place. Do you think I would return if I had a living elsewhere?"

So I told him that I had come back in the service of my country, and added that at the moment the dearest wish of my heart was to get out of it.

"It is easy neither to get in nor out, Sidney Georgevitch," said Alexander sadly. "Which way did you think of going?"

"I am trying to find someone who will bribe the station Commissar at Bielo 'ostrof to turn his back while I cross the bridge," I told him.

"It is no good," he said, shaking his head gravely. "Anybody else, perhaps—at a price. But you—no. Nobody in Russia *dare* let you go, however much you paid him. I recognised you. So will others. Perhaps you are not aware that at every station people are posted who know you. The rascals have traced you to Petrograd, and I may tell you that the Redskin who let you through the barrier was summarily shot. They are pretty certain that you have not left the city, and when they say that you seem to have escaped from Russia it is only to tempt you out of hiding. There are too many eyes watching, Sidney Georgevitch. No, we must think of some other way."

I could not but agree with him, especially since it had been proved so conclusively that my disguise was less effective than I had hoped it would be.

"Meantime," said the barber, "you are quite safe here. So far I have given no cause for suspicion. I have a clerical post in a Soviet Institution. If you will stay here I have an extra bed, and I shall be honoured by your company."

I stayed for about a fortnight with Alexander, and, having learned caution, did not venture out of the apartment. Nor did the house committee ever suspect my presence. As Alexander said, with a rueful glance round his bare room, they had taken all there was to be taken and so were not likely to trouble him again.

And during that two weeks Alexander was searching every channel for a means to smuggle me out of Russia.

Then one day he came in bringing with him a portly, heavy-faced man, who might have been a prosperous merchant or stockbroker—if such phenomena were to be found in Russia.

"Mr. Van den Bosch," said Alexander by way of introduction. The heavy-faced man bowed perfunctorily. "Mr. Van den Bosch is a Netherlander, who has come to Petrograd to do a little business with the Soviet Government. His boat—it is quite a small boat, a motor boat—lies in the river now."

Alexander paused to add emphasis. "I have explained to Mr. Van den Bosch your predicament
and your requirements. Mr. Van den Bosch is of
opinion that he might be able to help you."

I thanked the stranger in German.

"I understand," said Van den Bosch, "that you
are in some trouble with the government—such
government as it is in this country. What sort of
trouble it is is not my business to enquire. Of course
you will understand, Mr. ——"

"Bergmann," said I.

"You are a German?" (I bowed.) "Of course
you will understand, Mr. Bergmann, that my assisting you might very seriously prejudice my position. Not only would the very delicate trade
mission on which I am engaged be ruined, but I
would render myself liable to imprisonment for
assisting in the escape of a man who is wanted by
the authorities."

"Of course, I will make it worth your while," I
assured him. "How much do you want?"

"Sixty thousand roubles," said Van den Bosch.

"You shall have them."

"And when may I expect payment?" asked this
hard-headed business man.

"Half now and half when you land me," said I,
and counted out to him 30,000 roubles on the spot.

"I shall be sailing at midnight to-morrow," said
Van den Bosch pocketing the money. "Be early.
I cannot wait for you. Your friend here knows
where my boat is lying and will guide you to it. A

dinghy will be waiting by the quay. There will be no moon. But if you are followed don't try to come aboard."

Van den Bosch then left us. The following day I sent Alexander round to my old quarters, whence he succeeded in retrieving a suit and some linen in not too bad a state of disrepair. The faithful barber clipped my beard and moustache, and dressed my hair with a pair of rather blunt scissors. As a result I looked rather like a naval officer who had run a little to seed.

The good fellow then left me. We were to meet at 11 o'clock by the Kazan Cathedral. I was to board the boat at the last minute. A visit from the Bolshevik agents before she put to sea was almost inevitable.

The day seemed interminable. I amused myself by reading the copies of the Communist papers which Alexander had brought. I was not a little edified to find several references to myself and to the abortive conspiracy in which I had played a part. But there was little news. Most of the matter consisted of propaganda and the approaching war against the Imperialist powers of the West.

The night fell stormy and overcast. Great clouds were chasing one another across the sky and there were several downpours of rain. The streets were deserted when I set out for the ruined Kazan Cathedral.

Alexander was waiting for me. When he saw me he signalled a warning and slipped behind the hoarding which covered one face of the edifice. I joined him there.

"All is clear, Sidney Georgevitch," he whispered. "I have been down to the quay. The boat is waiting, as Van den Bosch promised. A Commissar has been on board with a soldier, but left at about eight o'clock. Since then the quay has been deserted. I will go ahead. If I see anyone suspicious I will pretend to stumble. That will be a signal to you to get under cover. If anything goes wrong make your way back to the Kamenostrovsky Prospekt. But go circuitously. You might be followed."

I let Alexander get some fifty yards ahead and then followed him. It had begun to rain hard much to my satisfaction. But I was drenched to the skin before we reached the quay. Nothing untoward had happened. Alexander stopped in the shadow of a large building and signalled me.

"Wait here," he whispered when I joined him. "All is not well. There is a light showing in the boat. Mr. Van den Bosch promised to show a light if you could not go aboard. Stay, while I go and investigate."

The faithful barber disappeared into the rain in the direction of the quay. By and by he returned looking anxious.

"The boat is showing a light, Sidney Georgevitch, and the dinghy is not at the quay as Van den Bosch promised. Something is wrong. We must return at once to the Kamenostrovsky Prospekt."

"Too late, Alexander. You have been followed."
Out of the downpour in the wake of the barber a
man had appeared, a giant of a fellow, who tow-
ered above myself and my companion in the uncer-
tain light. My hand closed on the butt of my revolver. My adventures seemed to have come to an
end at last. But a pleasant surprise awaited me.

"Herr Bergmann?" The newcomer addressed
me in German. "I am Mr. Van den Bosch's mechanic. I recognise your friend. I have seen him
with my master. Herr Bergmann, there is a Commissar on board the boat. You cannot come on
board until he leaves."

"And when does the Commissar intend to
leave?" I asked him.

"Not until the boat sails," said the mechanic.
"The Communists are suspicious about something.
A man came aboard yesterday night, when Mr.
Van den Bosch was away, and asked many questions. He was very anxious to know where Mr.
Van den Bosch had gone. And when Mr. Van den
Bosch returned he was followed. To-night the
Commissar came aboard again, and insisted on
examining each one of the crew. Mr. Van den
Bosch does not wish to offend the Bolsheviks. He
expects to do business with them. Therefore he is
entertaining the Commissar in his cabin until we
are due to sail. The Commissar has expressed the
polite intention of seeing us off and waving good-
bye from the quay."

"And when do we go aboard?"

"When the Commissar comes off."

"And if he sees us?"

"Herr Bergmann, the Commissar will not be in a condition to see anyone."

Sure enough, shortly after one o'clock the Commissar was brought ashore dead drunk. Hastily gripping Alexander's hand, I hastened across the quay with the mechanic and dropped into the dinghy.

Van den Bosch provided me with a change of clothing and some hot toddy. As I heard the screw thresh the water, a flood of exhilaration surged through me. I felt as a man feels who, after being almost suffocated, gets a breath of air. Slowly the rare lights of Petrograd dropped astern. Chug, Chug, Chug! In front of us was the open sea, Helsingfors, Copenhagen, England. At that moment running the gauntlet of the German naval base at Reval seemed but a minor risk. Chug, Chug, Chug! The drifting clouds were being chased out of the sky by the quickening breeze of morning. Here and there a watery star looked dimly down. Already the long grey fingers of dawn reached from the Eastern horizon. Chug, chug, chug! England, home, safety.

"Where are you bound for?" I asked Van den Bosch.

"The German Naval Base at Reval," was the answer.

Part Two

MRS. REILLY'S
NARRATIVE

Mrs. Reilly

THIS PHOTOGRAPH WAS CARRIED BY CAPT. REILLY AND IS POSTED AT
ALL RUSSIAN FRONTIERS FOR IDENTIFICATION PURPOSES

CHAPTER ONE

My first meeting with Sidney Reilly took place at the Hotel Adlon in Berlin. It was in the December of 1922, and the Reparations Commission was in session in the German capital. I was staying there with my mother and sister and among the acquaintances we made was an English delegate serving on the Commission.

The delegate was a charming man. He entertained us with many anecdotes of a singularly wide experience. And among other things he told us of Sidney Reilly. What heroic proportions the intrepid Intelligence Officer assumed as the delegate unfolded his story! How I trembled for his safety as the delegate said that even now this mysterious Mr. C. would go back to Russia—to that terrible Russia where he had thrice been condemned to death *in contumaciam*. There is something irresistible in such light-hearted courage, and I am not sure but that before even I met him I was dangerously interested in the fearless Mr. C.

I well remember the occasion when his name, or rather his *alias*, first cropped up in conversation.

"Do you know who is staying here?" asked the English delegate. "Mr. C., the man who only just missed smothering Bolshevism in its cradle. You have heard of him, Count?"

We were taking tea *à trois* in the lounge of the Hotel Adlon at Berlin, the British delegate, a German ex-naval officer and myself.

The German naval officer whistled.

"Mr. C., your ace of espionage? Heard of him? I should think I have. I have more than heard of him. I have seen him. I have spoken to him. I have dined with him. I have drunk with him. And all in the security of a German naval base during the war, when I was an officer in the German navy and he was a secret service agent in the employ of the British Government. Heard of him? Himmel! I should think I have. And he is actually staying here?"

"I saw him this afternoon," replied the British delegate, "but I could not get a word with him. But your story interests me, Count."

"I look forward to meeting him again," said the sailor. "What courage the man had—nerves of proved steel. And what a charming fellow with it. I give you my word, we were all pleased that he escaped, and, though the Admiral looked very grim when the news came through too late who he really was, I am sure that he was as pleased as the rest of us that the fellow had got away. It would have been our duty to shoot him, and one does not like to shoot a brave man."

"Who is this Mr. C.?" I asked.

"Who is he not?" asked the British delegate. "I tell you, Mrs. Chambers, this Mr. C. is a man of mystery. He's the most mysterious man in Europe.

And incidentally I should say he has a bigger price on his head than any man breathing. The Bolsheviks would give a province for him, alive or dead. Three times they have condemned him to death. The Lord alone knows how many times he has been in their clutches, if they did but know it. Why, I dare swear, seeing him in Berlin to-day, that he is fresh from Russia now, and is going back to-morrow. And Russia is not a healthy place to be in for anybody nowadays, even if he is not wanted by the Tcheka."

"Particularly if he's English," put in the naval officer.

"Then why does this Mr. C. go?" I asked.

"The exigencies of the service," said the delegate with a laugh. "He's a man that lives on danger. He has been our eyes and ears in Russia on many an occasion, and, between ourselves, he alone is responsible for Bolshevism not being a bigger menace to Western civilisation than it is at present. They put him over the frontier in Finland. It is ticklish work, I should say, dodging the Red patrols. Then he takes train to Petrograd, where all passports are examined. Ugh! I should not like to take the risk. But when did you last meet him, Count?"

"It was at Reval in 1918," said the naval officer. "He had just escaped from Petrograd after dodging a particularly nasty death there for a few months. I need not tell you that he had a price on his head in Germany too. We had put some of our best counter-espionage agents on him but without success. Well, one day a Dutch motor boat put into Reval with a Russian refugee on board. The Russian had got away in a hurry without a passport and without a change of clothes. But he had remembered to bring his moneybags with him. He became very popular at the naval base. He proved himself to be a most charming companion and made friends with many of our officers. Then one day he slipped away. Just in time too. Somebody had already suspected him, and the secret of his real identity reached us about twelve hours after he had gone."

It was the same evening that I had my first glimpse of Sidney Reilly, the man who was to be my devoted husband for two short years and then to vanish into the unknown. I need not say how the conversation between the British delegate and the German naval officer had fired my imagination, and the intrepid British officer assumed heroic proportions in my imagination, when raising my eyes from my coffee, I found them looking straight into a pair of brown ones at the other side of the room. For a moment his eyes held mine and I felt a delicious thrill run through me. The owner of the eyes presented a well-groomed and well-tailored figure, with a lean, rather sombre face, which conveyed an impression of unusual strength of resolution and character. The eyes were steady, kindly and rather sad. And with it all there was an expression, which might almost have been sardonic, the expression of a man, who not once but many times had laughed in the face of death.

All this was photographically impressed upon my mind during the second or two in which his gaze held mine. Then I looked away, wishing I knew somebody to introduce me to this fascinating stranger. I was not the only one who had noticed him. A small rat-faced man had followed him unobtrusively in and now sat in a corner whence he could command the chair in which the debonair stranger sat. I remember noticing with a sort of unreasoning irritation the keen curiosity of the rat-faced man. I suppose it was a sort of jealousy on my part, for of course at that time I did not attach any importance to the fact that the one man should watch the other so closely. Now I know that, wherever he moved, Sidney Reilly was being watched and dogged by the secret agents of the Tcheka.

Sidney, it appears, had been as attracted by me as I was by him. He had made up his mind at once that he must have an introduction to me. The task was not difficult for him. In a very short time he had found somebody to perform the ceremony. It was the British delegate who introduced Sidney to me.

Again his eyes met mine. Again a thrill ran through me. He stayed there talking to me, and his conversation fascinated me. He spoke of the state of Europe, of Russia, of the Tcheka, of the war, of Reval, and suddenly revelation came to me.

"You are Mr. C.," I said almost breathlessly, and ——

"Found out," said Sidney with a laugh.

Sidney always said that it was a case of love at first sight, and I do not think that he was far wrong. At the end of a week we were engaged.

Our engagement was a secret one, and I carefully kept it from my mother and sister during the short time that we were together. During that period too Sidney had little time to tell me of the work on which he was engaged. In a very short time he moved on to Prague and Paris. But a few weeks after we met again in London, whither I had returned to undergo an operation for appendicitis.

On May 18th, 1923, the very day that I left the nursing home we were married at the Register Office in Henrietta Street, Covent Garden, Sidney's old friend, Captain Hill, acting as a witness. And it is a strange enough commentary on human fame that in the accounts which appeared in the papers on the following day the interest was focussed on me, Pepita Bobadilla, the well-known actress, the widow of Haddon Chambers, the famous dramatist, rather than on the man, whose work behind the scenes of European politics had been so colossal, so important, so singularly unrewarded.

Sidney never spoke of his past achievements or adventures. Now and again there would be a passing reference in conversation—that was all. I might almost have thought that he wished to wipe entirely from his memory the horrors he had faced and survived, and finally to shut the door on all that part of his life with which they were connected. But it was not so. Not only was he devoted to the country of his origin, but he loved the land of his adoption. He lived in the present and the future. The experiences of the past were but incidents in a great campaign from which, as long as he lived, he would never for one moment rest, a campaign for the rehabilitation of his beloved Russia. The sole importance his past adventures had to him was the extent to which they could form a guide to his future activities.

Gradually I was initiated into those strange proceedings which were going on behind the scenes of European politics. I learned how beneath the surface of every capital in Europe was simmering the conspiracy of the exiles of Russia against the present tyrants of their country. In Berlin, in Paris, in Prague, in London itself, small groups of exiles were plotting, planning, conspiring. Helsingfors, the capital of Finland, was absolutely seething with the counter-revolution, which had been financed and abetted by several of the governments of Europe. In this whole movement Sidney was intensely interested and was devoting much time and money to the cause.

The great hope of the counter-revolutionists was Boris Savinkoff, who was living in Paris. This man was almost worshipped as a hero in many quarters, Sidney himself thought very highly of him and regarded him as the potential saviour of his country. Sidney had brought Savinkoff to the notice of Mr. Winston Churchill, who fully shared his opinion of him and always talked and wrote of Savinkoff as a great man.

Savinkoff was a firm opponent of despotism in any shape or form, and had been a strong and outspoken enemy of Tsarism. Of course the great majority of the counter-revolutionaries had been participators in or sympathisers with the first Russian Revolution. A short seven years before they had been revolutionaries themselves, and they naturally took Savinkoff as their leader. Sidney himself did not regard the restoration of monarchy in Russia as either feasible or desirable: he looked upon Savinkoff as the future dictator of the country. The Tsarists even were reconciled to the leadership of Savinkoff in the great crusade against Bolshevism. At the head of the Tsarists was a very able and brave man, General K., head of the Russian anti-Soviet Intelligence Department. In Russia itself, in Moscow and Petrograd, the counter-revolutionaries had their organisations in the charge of Savinkoff's aid, Pavlovsky, of whom more will be heard as my tale advances.

Of the White Russians as a whole Sidney did not have a very high opinion. He regarded them as vain, talkative and ineffective. They were full of words and schemes, but seemed incapable of translating their ideas into action. Many were undisguisedly apathetic, of many more the loyalty

was more than doubtful. As a class Sidney did not
regard them as reliable when outside his immediate control or supervision. From this general stric-
ture he excepted Savinkoff.

Savinkoff had been financed by the Polish,
French and Czech Governments, but, as time
passed, and nothing was done the interest of these
foreign sympathisers waned, and Savinkoff was
left to his own resources. He was now financed by
a few private individuals, among whom Sidney
was prominent, and, about the time of our marriage, Sidney was anxious to secure further support for him.

There can be no doubt that my husband had
the highest regard for Savinkoff, with whom he
had hoped to co-operate at the time of his abortive
conspiracy in 1918.

My husband's funds were not inexhaustible and
were much depleted by the advances he had made
to Savinkoff, but there was legally due to him a
large sum of money, part of which he intended to
use for further financing the Russian leader. This
dated back to before the time when he entered the
British Service. At the outbreak of the war he had
been sent to America by the Russian Government
to place contracts for arms and equipment. In this
work he had been highly successful, and it was in
this connection that a large sum of money was due
to him from an American firm. Owing to the
change of government in Russia, difficulties had
arisen with regard to the payment of this amount,

and my husband had now decided to institute proceedings for its recovery.

Accordingly almost immediately after our marriage my husband announced our pending visit to America. From London we went to Paris, where Savinkoff was living. It was amazing to what a degree some of his followers idolised this man. A self-constituted body-guard was watching over him very carefully. People who came to Paris to see him were watched and followed wherever they went. He did not see interviewers, who were received by his lieutenant, M. Dehrental.

On the face of them these precautions seemed a little melodramatic. As I was to learn, Sidney's life was in infinitely greater danger than Savinkoff's, and *he* went about absolutely unattended. But the fact is that the precautions were not entirely unnecessary. Unseen and hostile eyes were watching Savinkoff's every movement. The agents of the Tcheka never for one moment let him out of their sight. His residence was under an observation which slept neither night nor day. Shortly before our arrival in Paris we were told, an attempt had been made to kidnap him, which had been frustrated by the intelligence of the ubiquitous M. Dehrental. I remember that at the time I did not believe the story. And I am not sure that I believe it now.

However, be the truth of it what it may, there can be no doubt of the vigilance with which Savinkoff was guarded and the measures which were taken to keep his movements hidden. Sidney had announced by letter his impending arrival in Paris, and we were duly awaited by the secret agents. A message was sent at once to Savinkoff, and my first meeting with the great Russian hero took place in a private apartment of the Chatham Hotel.

Savinkoff was a great disappointment to me, though, knowing how much my husband admired him and regarded him as the hope of his country, I kept my unfavourable opinion to myself. A portly little man strutted in with the most amusing air of self-assurance and self-esteem—a little man with a high brow, a beetling forehead, little eyes and an undershot chin. The little man posed in front of the mantelpiece. Now he gave us a view of one side of his profile, now of the other. Now he thrust his hand into his breast in the approved Napoleonic manner, now he flourished it in the air with a theatrical gesture. Every pose was carefully studied, and had been studied so long that he had passed beyond the stage of taking even a glance at his audience to gauge the measure of its appreciation.

His little court fully shared Savinkoff's estimate of his own importance. When he frowned, a cloud settled on the assembly. When he smiled, answering smiles appeared on every face. When he condescended to a joke, which was but seldom, it was greeted with discreet and respectful merriment.

The conversation was conducted in Russian, which I did not understand. Dehrental did most

of the talking. Savinkoff attitudinised in the background. Dehrental became excited and gesticulated
wildly, but, whenever Savinkoff opened his mouth,
he subsided into respectful silence.

The conversation, as Sidney afterwards told me,
concerned itself principally with funds. Not only
was money badly needed for the counter-revolution, but subscriptions were in urgent request for
the keep of Savinkoff, together of course with that
of M. and Mme. Dehrental. The withdrawal of
the support of the French, Czech and Polish Governments had been a serious blow to the cause of
counter-revolution. Sidney had already pointed
out the danger of exhausting the patience of
friendly governments. The feeling was spreading
in Europe that, for all the White Russians could
do, Bolshevism had come to stay.

Dehrental produced reports from Pavlovsky and
the other counter-revolutionary agents in Russia,
from which it appeared that the time was not yet
ripe. His wife on the other hand seemed to be of
opinion that the sooner action was taken the better.
On only one point were they agreed, that funds
were urgently needed.

There was nothing more for my husband to do
in Europe and he was free to proceed to America
on his own affairs, which were causing him some
worry at this time. We sailed for New York in
July in the Holland-America liner *Rotterdam*.

At New York we stayed at the Gotham Hotel
for several months. A year passed uneventfully,

but Sidney was becoming more and more worried about his affairs. He made elaborate arrangements for my future in the event of his meeting with some mysterious accident, which he feared might befall him. At the same time he was assisting his friend, Sir Paul Dukes, in the translation of Savinkoff's last work, *The Black Horse*. The law delayed, and I saw that Sidney's health was suffering in consequence. Finally his lawsuit was postponed.

In the midst of all these perplexities came a letter from Savinkoff asking for Sidney's presence on a matter of grave importance.

In the summer of 1924 we sailed from New York on board the *Paris* and arrived in London.

CHAPTER TWO

I wakened suddenly from my sleep and sat up in bed. Sidney was standing in the moonlight of the window, looking out towards the Embankment. He seemed like a man in a dream. I went over and stood by his side, but he was not aware of me. He was looking, looking intently over the deserted drive, chequered with black shade and silver light, looking into the abysmal deeps of the shadows beyond. What was it at which he was gazing so intently? I too peered out shuddering, standing there by his shoulder, but he did not see me. Was it a hallucination? To my dying day I shall never know if it was a material thing I saw, as I stood there by Sidney's side, in the window in the moonlight. But as I peered, slowly looming out of the black shades I too seemed to see a grey shadow with face hideously cowled, looking across towards us, and beckoning, beckoning with arm slowly outstretched, beckoning with an air of irresistible command, beckoning to Sidney—beckoning to me, beckoning to both of us to come to it. In my terror I turned to Sidney, as he stood there, beside me, trying suddenly to hold him to me. But his face was unchanged and his eyes expressionless. He was asleep.

Again I turned my eyes fearfully to the window,

looking out over the deserted road. Again I strove to pierce through the black shadows. Nothing was there. As if to add to the air of normality a policeman was passing down, flashing his light on the doors of the houses as he went. Inside the room all was inky blackness. Sidney was breathing heavily, like a man in great distress. I led him gently back to the bed. He awakened there, and buried his face in my shoulder, sobbing like a child.

"Promise me one thing," he kept on saying to me. "Promise me one thing, that you will never go to Russia."

I soothed him and reassured him, as we sat there. "I promise," I said to humour his strange fancy. "I will never go to Russia."

"Whatever happens," Sidney went on, "however great the temptation, however plausible those that ask you, whatever promises are made. Even if I myself should write, asking you to come to me there. You must disobey. They are devils in the Tcheka," he went on almost to himself. "By one way or another they will get whom they want into their clutches, and, once there, no hope for him."

"Never be tempted into Russia." Oh, if Sidney had only remembered the warning he himself gave me so solemnly and awfully there in our rooms. His words remained in my mind and impressed themselves there. Never before or since did I see him, whose nerves were like strong steel, and whose courage and strength were unfailing, as indeed his manifold adventures testify, never before or since did I see him so shaken as he was on that night.

"Your husband is on the verge of a breakdown," the doctor told me. "Business worries. Can't you get him away from his business? Take him for a holiday somewhere—the south of France, the Mediterranean—anywhere—a complete change of surroundings. This imagining of things, restlessness, sleeplessness, somnambulism are quite common symptoms of an overwrought mind."

Imagining things? Should I tell the doctor what I myself thought I had seen, beckoning there from the shadows opposite our window? But everything seemed so normal with the daylight streaming into the room, and the noise of many people on the Embankment and all manner of tugs and shipping hooting and feeling their way down the river.

I laughed at the fears I had felt. A breakdown —yes, that was it. I was relieved. Even a breakdown was better than that cowled thing which had beckoned to Sidney from the shadows on the other side of the road. Sidney had been very worried over his business affairs lately. The adjournment of his law suit had depressed him. Besides, what dreadful adventures had he been through in the past? He never spoke of them himself, and had not then set on paper the narrative which is contained in the first part of this book, but Capt. Hill had told me of some of the things my husband had done. I did not tell the doctor of them however.

"Whatever you do," Sidney would say, "do not bring the service into it."

Sidney was quite keen when I broached to him the proposal of a holiday on the Continent. However, he had certain affairs which demanded his attention before he left London, and accordingly our departure was delayed for a few days, days which were to be among the most eventful in my life.

During the next week the feeling grew on me that we were being watched by unseen eyes, our every movement noted, and our comings and goings scrutinised. For some days I let the obsession grow on me, hiding it from Sidney as well as I could. But once again at midnight, being overwrought and unable to sleep, I slipped out of bed and went to the window—and, yes there in the same place, the mysterious figure was watching. A feeling of suffocation came over me. I longed to breathe free and pure air. Ah, that the business which still held Sidney in London might soon be over, that we might get away somewhere, far, far away, where the midnight watchers could not reach us.

It must have been about this time that the friend of my husband whom he mentions in his own narrative was spirited away from London. D.—my husband never told me of him, and I do not know his real name—was, I believe, one of the most prominent of Sidney's Russian agents in Moscow at the time of the hatching of the Lockhart conspiracy, and he was one of those people for whose sake Sidney made his heroic return to the city of the Terror after the assassination of Uritzky in Petrograd. D.'s wife had been murdered during the early days of the Terror, and he was one of the most persistent and relentless of the enemies of Bolshevism. He told nobody in London of his return to Russia, whither he was lured by the agents of the Tcheka.

I suppose it to have been just after this event that Sidney came in one day, looking unusually grave, and repeated the warning which he had given me before.

"Promise me that whatever happens you will never go to Russia. Even if I write asking you to come to me there, you must never go."

I gave the promise lightly. The contingency seemed so very remote. I asked his reason for exacting my promise.

"There are two or three people left, to be revenged on whom for services rendered the Bolsheviks would give their eyes. There are two or three people during whose lifetime the Bolsheviks will never sleep at peace. General Koutepoff is one. Then there is Boris Savinkoff. There are two or three others. The Bolsheviks will get them back to Russia if they can, and then —" Sidney spread out his hands in an expressive gesture.

I realise now that the man called D., who was lured back to Russia about this time, must have been one of those arch-enemies of the Bolsheviks,

one of those people who knew too much of the
inner workings of the terror of Eastern Europe
and would not rest until they had brought it crash-
ing to its ruin. Strangely enough, I did not realise
fully then that another of them, and the greatest
of them all, was my husband, Sidney George
Reilly.

As far as my memory serves me, it was on a
Tuesday that this conversation took place, and it
must have been on the Monday night that D. was
caught by the far spread tentacles of the Tcheka.

The next day the messenger of the Tcheka
arrived.

It was about eleven o'clock in the morning. Sidney and I were sitting together, making arrangements for our journey to France, which was now
quite settled for the following Friday. The servant
entered and announced to my husband that a Mr.
Warner had called and asked to see him.

Our visitor was shown in. In spite of his name
his appearance was anything but English. A tre-
mendous black beard almost hid his face, growing
right up to his prominent cheekbones, above which
a pair of cold and steely blue eyes probed first
Sidney's face and then my own. His build was
colossal, his shoulders high and massive, and his
arms were long and huge as those of a great ape.
Yet when he shook hands I noticed with a start
that his hands were long, refined, white and
delicate.

"I wished to see you privately," said this engag-

ing stranger to my husband. His voice was educated and pleasant to hear and he spoke without
trace of an accent.

"This is my wife," replied Sidney with a bow in
my direction. "I do not think that you can have
any business with me which she may not hear."

"As you like," said Mr. Warner with a slight
shrug, "though as a matter of fact the business on
which I have come is highly confidential." He
paused. "It is a political matter." Another pause.
"It is connected with Russia."

I saw a light leap to Sidney's eyes. I knew how
he hungered for news from that unhappy country,
how he still clung obstinately to the conviction
that the cause of civilisation was not yet altogether
lost there.

"Go on," said he, when our visitor paused again.
Mr. Warner looked towards me with an air of
puzzled enquiry. "Go on," repeated Sidney. "You
may speak in the presence of my wife."

Again the stranger bowed and shrugged.

"I have just come from Moscow and Petrograd."

"Ah!" escaped from my lips in an involuntary
sigh of realisation and apprehension. Mr. Warner
fixed me with a cold and hostile eye, as he resumed
his speech.

"I have just come from Moscow."

"And how are things there?" asked Sidney.

"As bad as bad can be," said Mr. Warner. "The
people are oppressed and are crying out for liberation. We want a *man* in Russia."

My gaze became riveted on Mr. Warner's left ear, which was not quite hidden in his voluminous beard. The ear impressed itself upon my notice. I remembered it accurately afterwards. It had apparently been frost bitten at some time or other and was disfigured in a singular manner.

"That was a fine organisation you had in Russia, Captain Reilly. We have picked up the strands again. We have got it working again. All your old agents are there. You remember Balkoff? he's with us. And Tuenkoff? And Alvendorff? And Vorislavsky? They are all working for us again. Some day or other we overthrow the Redskins, and the good times begin again. But—you know what we Russians are. We scheme and scheme and scheme, and build wonderful plot after wonderful plot, and quarrel among ourselves over irrelevant details, and golden opportunity after golden opportunity slips by, and nothing is done. Pah! it is enough to disgust a man with the whole thing. And all the time the valuable days are slipping by and nothing is done. You would weep, Captain Reilly, if you knew what wonderful chances we have had—and wasted. We are at a loss. We do not know what to do. When we have an idea we have not a man who has the courage and resource to carry it out. We want a man in Russia, Captain Reilly, a man who can command and get things done, whose commands there is no disputing, a man who will be master, dictator if you like, as Mussolini is in Italy, a man who will compose the feuds which disunite our friends there with an iron hand and will weld us into the weapon which will smite the present tyrants of Russia to the heart."

I saw Sidney's eyes kindling as the stranger spoke, saw the blood mounting to his cheek, saw his right hand clench and unclench. He was obviously deeply stirred. Excitement was surging up within him.

"When you went, Captain Reilly," Mr. Warner continued, "after your last visit to us, hope died within us. You cannot blame us. We had rank and file, men ready and eager for action, but we were leaderless. You cannot conceive what trouble it has been to build up our organisation once again. But we had no leader. We still have no leader. In our perplexity our organisation felt that it wanted advice, the advice of a strong proved man, who knew Russia. With one accord they all, Balkoff, Opperput, Alvendorff, Vorislavsky and the others called for you. It was agreed that one of us should come to England to see you and ask for—your advice. Behold we are ready to strike. We wait for the hand to guide us." Mr. Warner ceased with a gesture and a flourish.

"Who are you then?" asked Sidney.

"You do not know me, Sidney Georgevitch," said the other with an inflection almost of sadness in his voice. "And yet I know you. You remember how, when you were in Petrograd at a loss what to do, you were discovered by Alexander, who used to be in Maullé's saloon, and how he hid you in his house in the Kamenostrovsky Prospekt: you remember how after a fortnight he smuggled you away in a motor-boat belonging to a Mr. Van den Bosch, who brought you safely to Reval. Why do you think Alexander ran that great danger? Out of affection for you, because you tipped him generously in the old days? Bah! men do not put their neck in the noose for any such reason as that. It was I, Sidney Georgevitch, who recognised you in the street, and paid Alexander to take you into his care. It was I who arranged for Mr. Van den Bosch to come on a wildgoose chase to Petrograd after a business deal which nobody was contemplating. I had to work behind the scenes for reasons which—to you, who knew Red Russia—will be perfectly obvious. I could not meet you without bringing both of us into danger, and that is why I have not had the pleasure of meeting the gallant Captain Reilly until this moment."

"At least tell me your name, that I may thank you fittingly," said Sidney.

"Drebkoff," replied Mr. Warner simply. "Now head of the White Russian organisation in Moscow. I see that you still doubt me, Captain Reilly. See, here is my passport. I travel you will see as an Englishman born and a British subject. Do you still doubt me? See, here is a voucher written for me by Savinkoff, whom I saw in Paris. Here is a letter from V., with whom I conferred in Berlin. Here is a letter from Mr. X." (here Warner named a very prominent English statesman) "asking me to see him as soon as I arrive in London."

"These documents seem genuine right enough," said Sidney, examining one by one the papers, which our visitor threw upon the table. "Yes, this is Savinkoff's hand," he went on in a tone of increased respect, as he named the great hero and leader of the White Russians, for whom he entertained a particular veneration.

"Here," went on Drebkoff, "is a letter—a petition rather—to you from our friends in Russia, begging you, Captain Reilly, imploring you to join them in Moscow and lead just one more attempt, a successful attempt this time, to overthrow the tyranny of the Bolsheviks. Look what I have here. It is a Bolshevik passport made out for a certain Serge Ivanitch Konovaloff, an officer of the Extraordinary Commission. See, it is ready signed and sealed. Mark, there is the place for the photograph, and in my pocket is the official rubber stamp. See, here is the space for the description of the aforesaid Serge Ivanitch Konovaloff with not a letter yet filled in. At Helsingfors you will drop your British identity. Here is your Bolshevik passport. Captain Reilly, Russia is crying for you to come and lead her out of her captivity. As soon as you cross the border a million men will rally to your side. Come and be our leader. A whole great country is yearning for you to return."

It was at this stage that I spoke, still gazing at our visitor's deformed ear.

"My husband cannot go," said I. "He is unwell. The doctor has ordered him a complete rest. He cannot go to Russia."

I am afraid my little speech was rather a bathos following on Drebkoff's high-flown rhetoric. Its chilling effect was obvious and immediate. Sidney, who had been excitedly examining the papers which Drebkoff had brought, suddenly dropped them and straightened himself up, looking a little sad and wistful. Drebkoff shot a glance over towards me full of annoyance and hostility.

"My wife is quite right," said Sidney. "I should probably be worse than useless at the moment. I *do* need a rest, there is no gainsaying it. I have been overdoing things a bit lately. Afterwards, Drebkoff, you and our friends may count on me."

"We are ready now," Drebkoff answered with an air of sad submission. "Afterwards may be too late. Supporters melt away when they are kept waiting. Keenness gradually goes. Hope dies. Opportunity comes but once. Oh my unhappy country, my unhappy country. Nothing ever seems to go right."

Our visitor rose slowly to his feet with an air of such utter dejection, that for the moment I felt quite sorry for him.

"What will our friends say? What a terrible message I have to take back, what a blow to all their tenderly cherished hopes. I dare not face them with it. Captain Reilly, the one man in all the world on whom they thought that they could rely. Unhappy country! Unhappy people!"

"What about Savinkoff?" asked Sidney. "He is in Paris—the very man for you, a really great man, a great personality, a born leader and organiser."

I could read in Sidney's tone how great was the sacrifice he was making in handing over this business to Savinkoff, the Russian leader, whom he admired so wholeheartedly. But Drebkoff shook his head despondently.

"The people will not rally round Savinkoff as they would round you, Captain Reilly. No, he has not the name that you have. I will not detain you now. I shall be in London about a week, conferring with your Foreign Office. Perhaps, though my mission has proved abortive, you will do me the honour of lunching with me at the Savoy to-morrow."

With bowed head and chin sunk on his chest, Drebkoff walked dejectedly out.

On the following day Sidney announced that we would not go to France on the morrow. He had been in earnest consultation with Drebkoff over luncheon at the Savoy.

"The man seems quite genuine," Sidney told me afterwards. "About his papers there can be no doubt. He is staying in London about a week. It is not so long to wait. And I am anxious to learn fully what are the prospects of our friends in Russia."

Sidney's words fell on my ear like a knell, but I

hid my distress from him as well as I could. Why
I should have been suspicious of this Drebkoff at
that time I cannot say. But I was, and Drebkoff
sensed my hostility and did his best to placate it.
He invited us both to dinner with him on the Friday on which we should have sailed to France.

Drebkoff was the most thoughtful and charming
of hosts. The dejection which had sat upon him
when I last saw him had quite departed, and he
discussed the White organisation in Russia in
cheerful and optimistic tones. He spoke of its scope
and its potentialities, named its leading members
in Russia, and their prominent correspondents
abroad, and generally expressed himself most
hopefully of its future work. Not once did he recur
to the question of Sidney's accompanying him on
his return to Russia, whither he was bound as soon
as his secret political mission in London was
accomplished.

We spoke of other things, and Drebkoff showed
himself a man of wide culture and varied information. But somehow the conversation always went
back to Russia. Sometimes, it was Sidney who led
it back, sometimes Drebkoff. They had many mutual friends, and Sidney told me afterwards that,
though previously he had not met Drebkoff, he
knew his name as a member of one of the "Fives"
in my husband's widely flung organisation in Moscow. The evening passed quickly and charmingly,
and when I said Good-bye I felt half ashamed of
the suspicions I had entertained with regard to this

good-natured, bearded giant. But my suspicions had not entirely disappeared.

Sidney took every precaution. He wired to Savinkoff in Paris, and received from the Russian hero a most eulogistic account of the work of our visitor. The *bona fides* of Mr. Warner seemed established beyond cavil. And yet I remained suspicious of him, although I did not know then that behind my back he was using every sort of argument to persuade Sidney to reverse his previous decision not to return to Russia at the moment. But Sidney had promised me that he would not be persuaded, and all the eloquence, which, unknown to me, Drebkoff was pouring out day after day, was wasted upon my husband.

The week drew on to its end. Drebkoff was due to return to Russia via Finland. We were leaving London for Paris *en route* for Provence. I heaved a sigh of relief when our final preparations were made, our tickets bought, our places reserved in the train. The packing was finished, the luggage neatly stacked in the hall. Drebkoff had called to take formal leave of me, and was accompanied by Sidney to the station.

His going brought a great relief to me. I sat and awaited the return of Sidney. We were catching our train in the early afternoon. We would be in Paris the same night.

Then as I sat and waited there came a thundering at the door. A man stood there, hatless, coatless, breathless.

"Mrs. Reilly?"

"Yes."

"Mrs. Reilly, can you come with me at once? Your husband has met with an accident and has been badly injured."

He had not finished when I was putting on my hat, and asking a multitude of questions. Where was Sidney? Was he badly hurt? How did it happen?

"I have my car here," said the stranger. "He crossed the road just in front of me. I had not time to pull up. I cannot say whether he was badly hurt. They have taken him to a hospital. He was quite conscious. He asked me to come and fetch you at once." While the stranger was speaking, we hurried down to the road and entered a covered car which was waiting there. The chauffeur apparently already had his instructions, and no sooner had the door clicked behind my companion than we glided off towards the east.

The car was a deep one, and, what struck me as particularly strange when I had sufficiently recovered from my shock to take note of anything, all the blinds were down. Thus, though it was now nearly midday, we sat in semi-darkness, and I had no idea in what direction we were going.

"What hospital have they taken him to?" I asked my guide.

"It is quite close," he answered, evading a direct answer. "It won't take us more than ten minutes."

How long we had already been travelling I did

not know, for with the shock of the sudden news I had momentarily lost count of time. But we seemed to be moving fairly fast, and so far I had not noticed that we had encountered any serious traffic block. It seemed to me that the air inside the saloon was becoming unbearably stuffy and asphyxiating, and my nostrils seemed to detect a slight chemical smell.

At this moment the car turned sharply to the left with the result that my companion was thrown suddenly up against me, and at the moment I felt a sharp prick in my right arm. In a second it flashed through my mind that it was a hypodermic syringe. I was being kidnapped. I raised my hand and struck with all my force. Then the car seemed to slip away from under me and all was blackness.

Out of the pitch darkness which covered me beams of light seemed to glance and flicker. I seemed to be swinging round and round in a deep abyss: the light steadily grew brighter until it hurt my aching eyes.

"Ah! that is better," said a voice. A bespectacled old gentleman was regarding me anxiously. Behind his head I saw shelves and row upon row of bottles. I was sitting on a chair.

"Drink this," said the old gentleman, holding a glass to my lips. "You are all right. Don't be alarmed. Your husband has driven off to fetch a doctor."

I opened my eyes wide. The place I was in was obviously a chemist's shop. The chemist's assistant, a bovine-looking youth, was regarding me stolidly over the counter. The chemist himself was apparently the bespectacled old gentleman who had just given me a draught. In the open doorway a crowd of curious spectators was gathered.

"What happened?" I asked dully.

"Don't worry," replied the chemist in a soothing tone of voice. "You'll be all right now. You just came over faint in your car. Your husband has gone to fetch a doctor."

Then memory came back to me.

"I've been drugged," said I.

The chemist smiled in an exasperatingly sympathetic way.

"Don't worry," he kept on repeating, "you will be all right now."

My memory flashed back to the experiences of the last few minutes. Who had been the man who had attempted to carry me off? What had happened to Sidney?

"Have you a phone?" I asked. By way of answer the chemist repeated his exasperating formula.

"I wish to ring up my husband," I went on, and I gave him the telephone number.

"Your husband has gone to fetch a doctor," said the chemist.

"Fool, that was not my husband. Please ring up the number I have given you, and ask for Mr. Reilly."

With a patient air of humouring me the chemist did as I asked him, and by the time he had the number I was ready to take the receiver from him. My relief when I heard Sidney's voice on the phone may be imagined, although his tone was disturbed and anxious.

"I am just back from the station," he said, "and found your message waiting for me. I'm coming along at once."

"What message?"

"The man who knocked you down drove straight back here from the hospital." Of course I lost no time in reassuring Sidney on that point.

"The plan is obvious," said Sidney as we drove to the station that afternoon, "I was to be kidnapped and carried off to Russia. The best way to do it was to send me on a wildgoose chase after you. All that was necessary was to hide you away for a couple of hours. We were saved by a miracle. Do you know what the miracle was?"

"No."

"The hypodermic needle pierced your sleeve only. The injection did not go into your arm."

CHAPTER THREE

I feel sure that we were watched the whole way from London to Paris. Having seen to what length the Bolsheviks were prepared to go, I could have no doubt that, having so nearly had us in their clutches, they would not tamely submit to their defeat. The eyes with which I regarded what was probably a harmless old lady in the opposite corner of the railway carriage were dilated with fear and horror. Every stranger was charged with an indescribable menace. Sidney too was very much on the alert. I saw him scrutinise our fellow traveller very keenly. Once or twice he went out into the corridor and looked about him. He clearly suspected the presence of a hostile agent in the immediate vicinity.

On our arrival in Paris, Sidney was greeted by somebody whom he apparently knew. A small bearded man, obviously a Russian, was standing on the platform talking with a group of others when we alighted from the train. As soon as he saw Sidney he detached himself from his companions and came over to him, almost throwing his arms round his neck and apparently very excited at the encounter. They started talking rapidly in Russian together, while I took a hasty look at the group which Sidney's friend had just left. There were three of them, and they were all looking narrowly at Sidney. Then suddenly my blood froze in my veins. There in the group was Drebkoff. I could not doubt it. He had shaved off his beard. His hat was pulled well down over his eyes and his coat collar was turned up. He was so changed as to be almost unrecognisable, but there over his collar loomed one tell-tale ear, frostbitten and curiously distorted in the manner which, I felt, I would know anywhere. That it was Drebkoff I am absolutely certain. When he saw me he turned hastily away, and, whispering a word or two to his companions walked rapidly out of the station.

My feet and heart were like lead. Hours seemed to pass before Sidney had finished speaking to the little Russian. When he rejoined me I lost not a moment in telling him of what I had seen.

"I am not very afraid of Drebkoff at present," said Sidney. "I think the man was genuine enough. If he was not, it is bad for our organisation, because he obviously knew all about it from the inside. He told me things which he could only have heard from Pavlovsky or Savinkoff, and other things which I thought were known only to Savinkoff and myself. Savinkoff must trust him absolutely, and Savinkoff is not the sort of man to misplace his confidences."

"All the same," I replied, "I am certain that the man I saw was Drebkoff."

"Well, we will ask Savinkoff about him," said Sidney.

As it proved, however, we were not able to put the question to Savinkoff that night. The great Russian leader had been summoned to a conference by Mussolini, who apparently was prepared to lend Savinkoff the full weight of his financial support. The Italian dictator however had demanded a personal interview with Savinkoff first. So far, the two men had never met and negotiations between them had been conducted through an agent in Paris.

Mme. Dehrental was full of enthusiasm about the possible outcome of this meeting, and on Sidney too the news acted like a tonic. To satisfy me Sidney asked Mme. Dehrental whether she knew of Drebkoff. She had nothing but good to report of him. He was well known to Savinkoff, acted in close collaboration with Pavlovsky in Moscow, and was *bien vu* by both the French and British Foreign Offices.

The feeling that we were being watched by unseen eyes had followed me to Paris. That all visitors to Savinkoff's apartments were known we knew for certain. At dinner that night I felt that we were being closely scrutinised.

Savinkoff had been away from Paris more than a week when we arrived there, and we were not alone in awaiting his return. Mme. Dehrental introduced to us two Russians, who had arrived from the Moscow centre six days before, bearing an important letter from Pavlovsky to Savinkoff. The two men had taken obscure lodgings somewhere

and were in close hiding. Mme. Dehrental however had managed to see them every day. Sidney
questioned them both closely, but neither would
admit any knowledge of the contents of the letter
which they had brought to Savinkoff. Sidney then
tried to question them separately. He asked me to
engage the attention of the one, while he dealt with
the other. But it was no good. The two men could
not be separated. Everybody engaged in Russian
politics is suspicious of everybody else—and with
reason.

"The difficulty of this game," said Sidney with
a sigh, "is that you never know who is with you,
and who is against you. Many agents are taking the
pay of both sides."

The little man who had greeted Sidney at the
station, and whom I had seen talking to Drebkoff,
visited us at our hotel. Sidney did not tell him
where we were staying, but apparently he had no
difficulty in finding out. Once having found us,
there was no getting rid of him. He questioned me
about Sidney's movements, his intentions, his relations with Savinkoff, his hopes of the counter-
revolution, etc. He asked us for photographs of
ourselves, and was very distressed that we could
not supply him.

He had been one of the most seriously compromised of Sidney's Russian agents in Moscow in
1918, while ostensibly holding a responsible position in the Soviet Government. After the fiasco his
life had been in supreme danger, and the Tcheka

was hot upon his track. At great personal risk Sidney had got him out of Moscow disguised as a peasant woman, and after innumerable dangers he had escaped from Russia, by way of Archangel. Penniless in France he had been largely supported by Sidney. Surely if any man had cause to feel gratitude to another it was he.

Unfortunately of his treachery there could be no doubt. Having seen him with Drebkoff was enough for me. But there was other evidence against him. He was known to be in close touch with the Soviet Legation in Paris, and he was equally known to be trying to worm his way into the confidence of the man whom I will call Z. I do not give Z.'s full name because he is still alive in Paris, working in the counter-revolutionary cause there. Much will be heard of him in the course of my narrative.

I did not see Z. on the occasion of this visit, nor indeed for more than twelve months after, when my husband had already been betrayed to the Bolsheviks, and when he came forward to volunteer his assistance. But Sidney saw him frequently for a reason which I will now explain.

The reasons why Savinkoff had cabled to Sidney, why he was even now interviewing Mussolini, and why the emissaries of Pavlovsky were in Paris were as follows. A great counter-revolutionary plot was nearing completion. It was agreed that the moujiks would support any anti-Bolshevik campaign. The only difficulty consisted in transporting

an organised armed force to Russia. At this stage
Z. had come forward with a suggestion.

It is well-known that at this time—the summer
of 1924—a German scientist had perfected a
poison gas more horrible and more deadly than
any heretofore known. Z. claimed to be in touch
with this man, and able to get the formula from
him. A mere handful of men to manage the pro-
jectors would thus be all the expeditionary force
necessary. Sidney was to be in command. But to
start with, my husband was to go to Germany to
see the inventor, investigate the nature of the gas
and form of the projector, and thus be in a position to arrange for the transport to the Russian
frontier.

It is now my conviction for reasons which will
appear later that Z.'s story of the poison gas was
a pack of lies. However Z. seemed to be a very
keen worker in the cause and was trusted by Savinkoff. He was a man of culture and had enjoyed
a distinguished and adventurous career. He had
been a member of the Imperial Duma. He spoke
French, English and German fluently.

When we were out during the day our rooms at
the hotel were submitted to a systematic search.
Everything was gone through, but all to no avail.
It was obvious that somebody on the hotel staff was
in the pay of the Bolshevists, a fact which naturally
did not add to my peace of mind. Sidney's friend
of the railway station returned during the evening,
and asked many questions, particularly in relation

to Savinkoff: but Sidney let it be very clearly seen that he knew of our visitor's relations with the Soviet Embassy.

As a matter of fact in the Embassy itself Sidney had his ears. A woman employed there kept him *au courant* with the names of all the visitors to the Soviet ambassador. Among them was one whose name was unknown to us, but whose description I had occasion to remember afterwards. He was described as a tall, thin man with a deep scar which completely disfigured one side of his face.

Shortly afterwards this woman, Madame Schovalovsky, coming to see Sidney at the hotel, passed at the door his friend of the railway station. She recognised the man at once and realised that she herself was discovered. By the time that she reached our room she was almost fainting. Her terror was painful to witness. She was in despair. She was of opinion that no power on earth could save her from the vengeance of the Soviet, and in fact seemed to have lost even the will to save herself.

Sidney's resourcefulness however was equal to the occasion. Mme. Schovalovsky actually left the hotel in a packing case, in which she was conveyed to the house of a friend of my husband's. There her hair was cut short and, disguised as a man, she took up her residence in a flat in a poor quarter of Paris. She left Paris safely and went to New York, where we were to meet her again the following year.

Mme. Schovalovsky had brought us information of the greatest value and of a nature which I may not reveal. But she knew nothing of Drebkoff. With regard to this however I shall have more to say later.

My husband was closely watched, but no attempt was made upon him in Paris.

Savinkoff returned from Italy in a despondent mood. His negotiations with Mussolini had broken down. Probably the natural shrewdness of the Italian dictator made him suspect the sincerity of the would-be Russian dictator. Savinkoff himself represented the interview as a clash of strong wills. Mussolini was jealous of him as of a greater spirit. He gave us a very circumstantial account of their conversations together, in which it appeared that he had dictated to the dictator. I can see him now posing and attitudinising in front of the fireplace and delivering his words with a dramatic emphasis. The long and short of it was that he could get no financial help from Mussolini. The utmost the dictator was prepared to do was to provide him with Italian passports, and to instruct the Italian legation to render him personally every assistance in their power.

Sidney had almost ruined himself financially through assisting this man, and, failing a favourable outcome of his lawsuit, could not continue his remittances to him. I think that it was his failure with Mussolini, coupled with the knowledge that there was no more money to be had from his supporters, which determined Savinkoff on his next step, with which I now have to deal.

In his letter, which the two men from Moscow had brought, Pavlovsky stated that he had met with an accident, which prevented his coming to see his chief in person: he begged Savinkoff to return to Russia with the two men as his presence was absolutely necessary to the future welfare of the party.

Of the two men one was known to and trusted by Savinkoff, the other was a stranger. The letter was undoubtedly in Pavlovsky's handwriting. When Savinkoff had read out the letter, the eyes of all present—of Savinkoff, of the Dehrentals, of the two messengers—turned automatically to Sidney for his verdict.

"Don't go," said Sidney shortly.

The conversation was carried on in Russian. I did not know a word of the language. All I could do was to watch the varying expressions on the faces of each, and trace the course of the argument in that manner.

Sidney's jaw was set firmly and uncompromisingly. He said little, but whatever he said was concise and weighty. Savinkoff was thoughtful, now waxing expansive and spreading out his arms in dramatic delivery, now sinking his chin into his palm and keenly watching the others. Dehrental was worried, and seemed to shift his ground continually. Mme. Dehrental was voluble and persuasive, now pleading with my husband and

Savinkoff, now shooting a kindly and half-apologetic smile at the two messengers.

But it was these who particularly rivetted my attention. The one who was known to Savinkoff was white and trembling and had hunted and despairing eyes. The other, Andrea Pavlovitch, was grimly sardonic, and kept his eyes the whole time fixed on his companion. Terrible eyes they were, cruel, cold and piercing. Somehow he reminded me of a cat playing with a mouse. As I watched I could have no doubt of the mission of these men. The one who was known to Savinkoff had come under the stress of some terrible threat: if he betrayed his employers there was no help for him: even in the security of civilised Paris the tentacles of the Tcheka were coiled round him. But to make assurance doubly sure an agent had been sent with him to see that he did not give the show away once he was out of the country. As for Pavlovsky, either he had turned traitor or the accident which had befallen him was simply the torture to which he had been put to compel him to write the letter.

Such were the conclusions to which I came on that night, and with a few modifications I adhere to them now. Sidney confirmed my view of the course of the discussion. His attitude had been throughout "have nothing to do with it. It is a provocation." Savinkoff was in doubt, although he trusted Pavlovsky absolutely. Mme. Dehrental however had come out whole-heartedly on the side of the messengers, and had declared her willingness to return to Russia without more ado. Remembering that she had seen the *provocateur*, Andrea Pavlovitch, daily for more than a week while Savinkoff was away in Italy, I was not surprised. I gave it as my opinion that the woman had been bought by the Bolsheviks.

Sidney agreed with my conclusions, but in view of the relations between Savinkoff and Mme. Dehrental he could not communicate his suspicions to the Russian leader. Mme. Dehrental however, with the sharp intuitiveness of her sex, realised at once who her enemies were.

Night after night we met and continued the discussion. Sometimes Pavlovsky's messengers were present, sometimes not. By no means could we get them apart.

One discussion was very much like another. Sidney was obdurate, Savinkoff dubious. Dehrental became more and more worried, his wife more and more voluble. I could almost see the cold perspiration standing out on the forehead of Pavlovsky's aide, as with trembling lips he tried to be persuasive. And all the time Andrea Pavlovitch was watching him with grim sardonic eyes, as a cat watches a mouse, and ready to pounce if he said one word wrong. Andrea Pavlovitch left all the talking on their side to be done by his companion. When appealed to himself, he would shrug his shoulders or grunt out two or three words at most.

One day Mme. Dehrental rang up Sidney, instructing him from Savinkoff not to meet him that day, as he was being closely watched and there might be danger. Sidney calmly disregarded the instructions and we appeared as usual. Never shall I forget the twinkling malice in Mme. Dehrental's eyes when she saw us. Somehow or other she and Andrea Pavlovitch wished to get us out of the way, while Savinkoff was being persuaded.

It took Savinkoff about three weeks to make up his mind. At the end of that time he was resolved to return to Russia with the Dehrentals and the two messengers. Dehrental himself continued to look very worried. He obviously did not like the look of the thing at all. So convinced was I that the whole thing was a trap that I begged Dehrental to arrange for Savinkoff to have a small accident, which would prevent his going. It was not to be. On August 10th, after a final long conference with my husband, Savinkoff equipped with an Italian passport and accompanied by the Dehrentals and the two messengers, left for Russia by way of Berlin.

The utmost precautions were taken to ensure that his identity should not be disclosed, or his safety endangered. He was to send a message to Sidney as soon as he could with safety. In those terrible times in Russia that might mean weeks. The days passed and no message arrived. How great the suspense was I need not say. The strain for Sidney was colossal. But no news was so far good news, that if he had really been lured into a trap and captured by the Bolsheviks we should have heard of it by now. As a matter of fact, when the first news arrived our suspicions with regard to the whole business had almost sunk to sleep, and Sidney's chief anxiety was lest Savinkoff might be discovered by an accident.

The first news we had came as a terrible shock. It was an announcement in the official Bolshevik journal, the *Isvestia*, for August 29th that Savinkoff had been arrested in Russia. But what was that to the news which rapidly followed: first that he had been condemned to death: then that the sentence had been commuted to ten years' imprisonment: then that he was completely acquitted: finally that he was a free man again. The natural conclusion at which the anti-Bolshevik Press arrived was that Savinkoff's reconciliation with the Bolsheviks had taken place before ever he left Paris.

On this Sidney wrote a letter, which was published in the *Morning Post* of September 8th, 1924. I quote it in full because it shows the extent of his loyalty to Savinkoff, because it is a revelation of the Tcheka methods from one man in all the world who was most qualified to discuss them, and finally because the fate which he supposed to have befallen Savinkoff affords a remarkable analogy to his own mysterious doom twelve months later.

SIR,

My attention has been drawn to the article, "Savinkoff's Nominal Sentence", published in the *Morning Post* of September 1. Your informant, without adducing any proofs whatsoever and basing himself merely on rumours, makes the suggestion that Savinkoff's trial was a "stunt" arranged between him and the Kremlin clique, and that Savinkoff has already for some time contemplated a reconciliation with the Bolsheviks.

No more ghastly accusation could be so carelessly hurled against a man whose whole life has been spent fighting tyranny of whatsoever denomination, Tsarist or Bolshevist, and whose name all over the world has stood for "No Surrender" to the sinister powers of the Third International.

I claim the great privilege of being one of his most intimate friends and devoted followers, and on me devolves the sacred duty of vindicating his honour. Contrary to the affirmation of your correspondent, I was one of the very few who knew of his intention to penetrate into Soviet Russia. On receipt of a cable from him, I hurried back, at the beginning of July, from New York, where I was assisting my friend, Sir Paul Dukes, to translate and to prepare for publication Savinkoff's latest book *The Black Horse*. Every page of it is illumined by Savinkoff's transcendent love for his country and by his undying hatred of the Bolshevist tyrants. Since my arrival here on July 19th, I have spent every day with Savinkoff up to August 10, the day of his departure for the Russian frontier. I have been in his fullest confidence, and all his plans have been elaborated conjointly with me. His last hours in Paris were spent with me.

Nineteen days later came the news of his arrest, then in quick, almost hourly, succession, of his trial, his condemnation to death, the commutation of the death sentence to ten years' imprisonment, his complete acquittal, and finally his liberation.

Where are the proofs of all this phantasmagoria?

What is the source of this colossal libel? The Bolshevist News Agency "Rosta"!

It is not surprising that the statements of the "Rosta," this incubator of the vilest Bolshevist *canards*, should be swallowed without demur, and even with joy, by the Communist Press, but that the Anti-Communist Press should accept those palpable forgeries for good currency is beyond comprehension.

I am not yet in a position to offer you definite proofs of this Bolshevist machination to discredit Savinkoff's good name; but permit me to call your attention to the following most significant facts:

1. The "Rosta" states that Savinkoff was tried behind closed doors. We must assume that no correspondents of non-Communist European or American papers were present, otherwise the world would have already had *their* account of the proceedings.

2. The official Bolshevist journal, the *Isvestia*, up to August 28, does not mention a single word about Savinkoff. Is it likely that having on the 20th achieved such a triumph as the capture of their "greatest enemy" the Bolsheviks would pass it over in silence during an entire week?

3. What do all the so-called "sincere confessions and recantations" consist of? Of old political tittle-tattle which has been known for years to every European Chancery and also to the Bolsheviks, and has now been rehashed for purposes of defamation and propaganda. Not a single new and really confidential fact as regards Savinkoff's activities or relations with Allied statesmen during the last two years has come to light.

4. No confederates are either mentioned or implicated in the trial with Savinkoff. What are the inferences to be drawn from all the above facts?

Savinkoff was killed when attempting to cross the Russian frontier, and a mock trial, with one of their own agents as chief actor, was staged by the Tcheka in Moscow behind closed doors.

Need one mention the trials of the Socialist Revolutionaries, of the Patriarch, of the Kieff professors, in order to remind the public of what unspeakable villainies the Bolsheviks are capable? For the moment they have succeeded in throwing a shadow on the great name of their admittedly most active and most implacable enemy. But truth will penetrate even the murky darkness of this latest Tcheka conspiracy, and will shine forth before the world. Then it will be seen that of all men who in our time have combated the Moscow tyrants, none had a greater right to Victor Hugo's proud assertion: *S'il ne reste qu'un—je le suis!*

Sir, I appeal to you, whose organ has always been the professed champion of Anti-Bolshevism and Anti-Communism, to help me vindicate the name and honour of Boris Savinkoff.

Yours, etc.,
SIDNEY REILLY.

At the same time he wrote to Mr. Churchill to the following effect:

DEAR MR. CHURCHILL,

The disaster which has overtaken Boris Savinkoff has undoubtedly produced the most painful impression upon you. Neither I nor any of his intimate friends and co-workers have so far been able to obtain any reliable news about his fate. Our conviction is that he has fallen a victim to the vilest and most daring intrigue the Tcheka has ever attempted. Our opinion is expressed in the letter which I am to-day sending to the *Morning Post*. Knowing your invariably kind interest I take the liberty of enclosing a copy for your information.

I am, dear Mr. Churchill,
Yours very faithfully,
SIDNEY REILLY.

3rd September, 1924.

To this Mr. Churchill replied as follows:

Chartwell Manor,
Westerham, Kent.
5th September, 1924.

DEAR MR. REILLY,

I was deeply grieved to read the news about Savinkoff. I do not, however, think that the explanation in your letter to the *Morning Post* is borne out by the facts. The *Morning Post* to-day gives a fuller account of the procès verbal, and I clearly recognise the points we discussed at Chequers about free Soviet elections, etc. You do not say in your letter what was the reason and purpose with which he entered Soviet Russia. If it is true that he has been pardoned and liberated I should be very glad. I am sure that any influence he could acquire among those men would be powerfully exerted towards bringing about a better state of affairs. In fact their treatment of him, if it is true, seems to me to be the first decent and sensible thing I have ever heard about them.

I shall be glad to hear anything further you may know on the subject, as I always thought Savinkoff was a great man and a great Russian patriot, in spite of the terrible methods with which he has been associated. However it is very difficult to judge the politics in any other country.

Yours very truly,
WINSTON S. CHURCHILL.

Very soon there could be no doubt that the accounts which had appeared in the *Isvestia* were true in substance. Savinkoff had betrayed his friends, his organisation, his cause, his country, and had sold himself body and soul to the enemy. The news was a terrible shock to Sidney, to whom Savinkoff had always been an object almost of hero-worship.

It was with a heavy heart that Sidney once again took up his pen and wrote to the *Morning Post* a retraction of his former letter.

SIR,

I once more take the liberty of claiming your indulgence and your space. This time for a twofold purpose, first of all to express my deep appreciation of your fairness in inserting (in your issue of the 8th inst.) my letter in defense of Boris Savinkoff when all the information at your disposal tended to show that I am in error; secondly, to perform a duty, in this case a most painful duty, and to acknowledge the error into which my loyalty to Savinkoff has induced me.

The detailed and in many instances stenographic Press reports of Savinkoff's trial, supported by the testimony of reliable and impartial eye witnesses, have established Savinkoff's treachery beyond all possibility of doubt. He has not only betrayed his friends, his organisation, and his cause, but he has also deliberately and completely gone over to his former enemies. He has connived with his captors to deal the heaviest possible blow at the anti-Bolshevik movement, and to provide them with an outstanding political triumph both for internal and external use. By his act Savinkoff has erased for ever his name from the scroll of honour of the anti-Communist movement.

His former friends and followers grieve over his terrible and inglorious downfall, but those amongst them who under no circumstances will practise with the enemies of mankind are undismayed. The moral suicide of their former leader is for them an added incentive to close their ranks and to "carry on."

Yours etc.,
SIDNEY REILLY.

This brought a second letter from Mr. Churchill.

Chartwell Manor,
Westerham, Kent.

15th September, 1924.

DEAR MR. REILLY,

I am very interested in your letter. The event has turned out as I myself expected at the very first. I do not think you should judge Savinkoff too harshly. He was placed in a terrible position; and only those who have sustained successfully such an ordeal have a full right to pronounce censure. At any rate I shall wait to hear the end of the story before changing my view about Savinkoff.

Yours very truly,
W. S. CHURCHILL.

Savinkoff wrote my husband long letters from prison, explaining his action, excusing himself and defending the Bolsheviks. But my husband never answered them. The treachery of his old friend was as big a blow as he could stand.

We sailed for New York in the *Nieuw Amsterdam*. The Bolsheviks had won the first round.

CHAPTER FOUR

The interest of the Bolsheviks did not wane when we left Europe. I noticed that one of the stewards was watching us very closely, so closely that he attracted my attention. He was a tall, shaven man, whom I would not have recognised but for his ear, which was disfigured in a peculiar manner. It was Drebkoff.

Sidney was carrying important papers with him and he was practically certain that some attempt would be made by the Bolsheviks to get them. During his stay in Europe he had been implicated in a very important political transaction, the details of which I am not at liberty to divulge. But the result was that a great deal of importance attached in Bolshevik eyes to his attaché case.

I got into conversation with Drebkoff but he carried out his part with the most amazing impudence. He all but admitted his identity. He was a Russian working his way to America. He knew all about Sidney and had seen him often in Petrograd. He gave his name as Constantine.

"He is a little too obvious," was Sidney's comment. "Our real watcher is probably somebody quite different."

In the lounge Sidney met another Russian acquaintance. (These Russians seem to be everywhere, I thought despairingly.) This was a small man with an artificial limb, having left one leg on the battlefields of his country. He was now resident in America and was a worker and lecturer in the anti-Bolshevik cause.

"Would you know that man again if you saw him?" Sidney asked me one day.

"Yes, I think so. Why?"

"That is the real agent. The steward is only a blind."

"But why do those men come to America?" I asked him. "Is it merely to follow you?"

"Not entirely," said Sidney with a laugh. "The Soviet is trying to raise a loan in America. Apart from their official representatives they are employing a large number of secret agents. When this man lands he will blossom out as a convert to Bolshevism. He is quite well-known in America for his anti-Bolshevik work, and his conversion is bound to have some influence."

This example of duplicity, following so closely on the Savinkoff affair, astounded me, and I found it very hard to believe. But Sidney was right. There were constant comings and goings between the two camps, and it was difficult at any given time to say who were your friends and who were your enemies. With a few significant exceptions there seemed to be no such thing as gratitude among the Russians.

The weather was fine and the ship comfortable, but all the same it was a great relief to me when

the journey was over, and I was as glad to see the
statue of Liberty coming nearer and nearer as a
few months afterwards I was to see the last of it.

A reception committee greeted us when we
landed. The colony of Russian refugees in New
York is not a small one, and it was well represented
in the group of people who welcomed us. Among
them was Marie Schovalovsky. She was now living
in New York. So great was her fear of Bolshevik
retribution that she had changed her name. How
she had managed to settle in America without her
name having been on the immigration quota list I
do not know. The Russian refugees had influential
friends in America, and no doubt influence had
been brought to bear.

Even in New York Mme. Schovalovsky was in
mortal terror of the retribution of the Tcheka. She
refused categorically to take part in any anti-
Bolshevik work. She lived in obscurity and gave
no one her address. She had not only changed her
name but her appearance too as far as she could.

She was able to identify the scar-faced man at
once from my description. She did not know his
name, but knew him as an agent of the Tcheka.
The news that he had crossed the Atlantic filled
her with dire alarm. She was sure that he had come
to "liquidate" her, as the cant Bolshevik term has
it. Sidney's opinion, however, was that the scar-
faced man had crossed to New York on espionage
work in connection with the loan which the Union

of Soviet Socialist Republics was endeavouring to float in the United States.

The Russians in New York are of the better class, and for the most part are financially independent. The artisans of that race are almost without exception emigrants from pre-war Russia. Some of them are infected with Bolshevism. The refugees, being comfortable from the material point of view, are content to let well alone, and take no part in Russian politics. Even so strenuous attempts have been made to disseminate Bolshevik doctrine in the States, and the international revolutionary Lodge has a powerful branch there. Many Americans take an impartial interest in Bolshevism. Moreover there are, of course, in America many shrewd business men, who are not much concerned with principles or politics as long as they can see a good return for their money. There was an excellent chance of a good return from a country of the vast undeveloped resources of Russia. In short the prospects were bright of the Soviet being able to float its loan. Sidney was determined that it should not. A great part of his work in America was to be aimed at frustrating that loan.

The interests of the average American are catholic and insatiable. His taste for lectures is inordinate. Both by public lectures and by articles in the Press Sidney fought against the Bolshevik loan. And it is needless to state how by revelation after revelation, by discovery after discovery he won a complete victory, and the Soviet loan never materialised.

The Bolsheviks on their side used every endeavour to convince America of their honesty and the humanity of their *régime*. I quote an article which appeared in the *New York American* of February 16th, 1925.

"MOSCOW, FEBRUARY 15TH.

The Soviet Government formally and officially set out to prove that the era of vengeance and of terror is a thing of the past in the history of the Russian Soviet by throwing open the chief G.P.U. prison to inspection by foreign newspaper-men for the first time.

Yagoda, chief of the G.P.U. and successor of Dzerjinski, who directed the injurious methods of dealing with political opponents long popular in Russia, declared Russia had nothing to conceal. He said to-day:

'Now that the counter-revolution is of the past, we have only about eighty political prisoners.

'We pursue the most humane and liberal methods, giving the prisoners physical and moral comforts. We have parted definitely with the policy of vengeance. Our prison system is of the best, despite foreign lies. We are admitting foreign correspondents because we have nothing to hide. Let all doubters come and see for themselves.'

The correspondents were conducted through the building, formerly a first-class hotel, in Loubianka Square. It still bears traces of its ancient comforts, in parquet floors and big, light rooms, well ventilated. Sanitary conditions prevail and the food is wholesome.

The chief point of interest was the room where General Savinkoff is held. He has a very comfortable room and devotes his time to writing fiction.

The General said he preferred prison to Polish or Czecho-Slovakian hospitality, as he likes to breathe the air of Russia, if only through the bars of a prison."

The details about Savinkoff of course interested us vastly, and I was hugely amused to picture him there as great a poseur and attitudiniser as ever, mouthing to the world his patriotic platitudes from his prison.

Meantime the lawsuit which had brought Sidney to America at last came on for hearing, and it is necessary at this stage for me to state exactly what the case was.

Sidney Reilly, as has previously been mentioned, had been sent by the Imperial Russian Government to New York to arrange ammunition contracts for the Russian army. When the Russian Monarchy fell these contracts were taken over by the British Government, on the condition that no agreements for commission existed. At that time Sidney held an agreement for commission amounting to half a million dollars. An officer of the company asked Sidney to cancel the agreement in order that the company might accept the British Contract. This officer, who was a personal friend of my husband's, assured him that the commission would be paid in full even if he had to pay it out of his own pocket. Sidney took his word that his interests would be guarded even without the agreement, which he tore up.

The official was a shrewd business man. When the time came he refused to pay and the lawsuit was started. The defence was admirable in its impudence. It was not denied that the agreement had existed, nor asserted that the company had given Sidney any compensation for its cancellation. The case put before the court was that Sidney destroyed a valuable contract without any consideration whatsoever.

On the advice of his solicitor Sidney's case was made a suit for damages for misrepresentation, and was accordingly tried before a jury. The jury consisted of artisans. Instead of confining himself to the relevant points at issue counsel for the defence dwelt at great length on Sidney's anti-Bolshevik work, and the campaign against the Soviet which he was even then waging. The case was judged before it was heard, and Sidney was cast in his suit. Not another court in the world would have returned such a verdict.

The Bolsheviks lost no opportunity of keeping themselves *au courant* with my husband's activities. He had taken an office in Broadway, and in the next suite another firm established itself. It soon became obvious that there was a serious leakage. Photographic reproductions of papers were finding their way into the hands of the Bolsheviks. Sidney set a trap, as a result of which his Russian secretary, Mlle. G., was found guilty of opening Sidney's correspondence, photographing the contents and resealing the letters. Thereafter for almost a year all the papers which were accessible to Mlle. G. were carefully prepared beforehand,

and the information which found its way to Russia was in the highest degree misleading.

All this of course entailed a great deal of extra work. All vitally important political matters, and the doctoring of the papers for the benefit of Mlle. G. were attended to in our own rooms at night. And thus I became a sort of additional secretary to my husband, and learned more and more of the activities of the anti-Bolsheviks throughout the world.

It is important to realise that by far the greater part of the active anti-Bolsheviks had themselves been revolutionaries, and many of them exiles from Tsarist Russia. The Bolsheviks themselves had very carefully kept their own necks out of danger, and only returned to Russia when the Social Revolutionaries had succeeded in overthrowing the monarchy. The chief Social Revolutionaries were themselves now in exile, and formed the backbone of the anti-Bolshevik cause. The *émigrés* proper played very little part in politics, and were generally quite content to exercise their talents in that profession to which the revolution had reduced them.

Anti-Bolshevism received several accessions of strength from the ranks of the Soviets themselves, but these deserters came to be regarded with a great deal of suspicion. As often as not, after enjoying the hospitality and sharing the councils of the anti-Bolsheviks, they returned to their old allegiance with a great deal of valuable information gathered during their exile.

The great difficulty was then, and remains now, to get the anti-Bolsheviks to combine. There are many mutual jealousies and mutual suspicions. Organisations are mutually exclusive. The greater number of them were quite content to adopt the Micawber attitude of waiting for something to turn up. Others were active only in endeavouring to secure the intervention of foreign powers. After Savinkoff's betrayal and the subsequent dispersal of the "Greens"—the organisation with which he had been connected—we were in touch with no organisation operating in Russia itself.

Sidney very rightly saw that the counter revolution must start in Russia, and that all his work from the outside world would only result in creating a passive foreign hostility to the Soviet. He was approached several times on behalf of organisations in Moscow, as he had been approached by Drebkoff in London, but he proceeded very warily, and inevitably found these organisations to be controlled by Bolsheviks, whose apostasy was more than doubtful.

Meanwhile he received several anonymous letters warning him to discontinue his anti-Bolshevik work, and the Soviet spies in New York continued to keep him under close observation. Our rooms were ransacked more than once, and of course it was out of the question to inform the police. But the honours of the duel were very easily with

Sidney. He bluffed his enemies continually and managed to surprise from them a considerable amount of valuable information of which he knew how to make use.

It is well known that the Bolsheviks have spent a great deal of money in order to foment revolution in other countries. Papers and revolutionary bodies were subsidised by them, but as a result of my husband's espionage work foreign chancellories were kept posted with intelligence of this side of Bolshevik work. At every turn he was impeding the operations of the Bolsheviks. The Soviet recognised in him their most dangerous and courageous enemy and sighed to be able to put into execution the death sentence which they had passed on him in his absence seven years before.

In the meantime, however, his business affairs did not prosper. Things gradually grew worse and worse. At last he could justifiably dispense with the services of Mlle. G.—but only after she had been of great, if unwitting use to him.

About this time we received a call from Mme. Schovalovsky. Until now she had not been near us owing to her intense fear of the Tcheka and the revenge she was sure the Bolsheviks were preparing for her. This woman was the daughter of a professor of languages at Moscow. She had been attached for a time to the Soviet Embassy in Paris, and her father, a convert to Communism, had remained in the Russian capital. Following her flight from Paris he had been arrested on a charge of

complicity and imprisoned in the Loubianka, and
Mme. Schovalovsky was greatly perturbed about
his fate. Now, however, she had received a letter
from him saying that he was seriously ill and imploring to see her again before his death. The letter hinted at many things, and suggested that he
had been wounded while effecting his escape, and
that he was lying in a dangerous condition at the
house of a friend in Moscow. It was unlikely that
he would live long, or that he would be able to
travel far, otherwise he would make some attempt
to come to America and see his daughter before he
died.

Mme. Schovalovsky was distraught. What was
she to do? She waited anxiously for further news.
When it came it brought her round to Sidney for
advice. The old man wrote imploring her to return
to Europe. He might be able to escape from Russia and meet her in Paris or Berlin. "Shall my old
eyes never behold you again?" he wrote. "I fancy
you near me sometimes, and that I can see your
dear mother's head, as she dozes in her chair. Am
I never to see my child before I die? God's will
be done." And this time he enclosed some money.
It was enough for her passage.

The thought of her old father lying untended in
Moscow was altogether too much for Mme. Schovalovsky. Yet she feared to return. What was she
to do? Sidney was of opinion that she would be
quite safe as long as she did not enter Russia itself.
Berlin was nearer to the frontier indeed but not

more dangerous than New York. Long and earnestly we discussed the question between us. And in the meantime another letter arrived from her father, asking When are you coming?

Mme. Schovalovsky's mind was made up. She would return to Europe, and endeavour to get her father out of Russia. Sidney gave her letters of introduction to friends in Berlin, and instructed her to ask their advice, before admitting any change in the plans which we formulated together. She was to wait in Berlin, and make no attempt to see her father unless he could be brought to her there.

So Mme. Schovalovsky set sail, and in due course we heard from Sidney's friends in Berlin of her arrival there. From there she proceeded to Warsaw, where she was to meet her father and herself conduct him to Berlin.

We heard from Sidney's friend in Berlin of her going to Warsaw and of the reasons for it. A message had reached her at Berlin that her father lay desperately ill, and that the friends who were hiding him could guarantee only to bring him as far as Warsaw. At Warsaw apparently it was the same story and Mme. Schovalovsky proceeded to the frontier. She was never heard of again.

Several possibilities present themselves with regard to the fate of Mme. Schovalovsky, all of which are consistent with what we know of the Bolshevik methods.

(1) Her own father might have acted as a provocation agent and used her affection for him to lure her back to the vengeance which awaited her.

(2) The friends, who hid him, might have done so only as part of the scheme by which the Soviet was to achieve its revenge.

(3) The correspondence which passed between them might have been opened and read from the start by the Tcheka.

The circumstances of her disappearance and the fact that her "friends" played into the Bolsheviks' hands render the two former possibilities more likely.

Sidney had a complete list of those who were secretly working for the Bolshevik cause in America. In obtaining it I played my part for the first time in espionage work. Mlle. G. was our unknowing ally.

As soon as Sidney knew that Mlle. G. was forwarding copies of his letters to her employers, he wrote a letter to a friend, in which he stated that he was meeting a wealthy American, whom he designated by an initial, at such and such a café at such and such a time. He went on to say that the American was prepared to finance a great anti-Bolshevik scheme, on which Sidney was engaged. Needless to say, this American had no real existence, but Sidney knew that the Bolsheviks would be exceedingly anxious to find out the identity of

this supposed ally of my husband's. In the circumstances he would be closely watched in the
café, and by the exercise of a little care should be
able to pick out whoever was spying on him.

Accordingly at the time fixed Sidney took up
his position at a table where he could command
the whole of the room. I was to join him at the end
of half an hour, when he had made his obser-
vations.

At the end of the half hour I came and sat at
his table and Sidney gave me a minute description
of the man who was watching him. Meantime my
husband kept on consulting his watch, and finally
gave me a note, with which I ostensibly departed.

Just outside the entrance to the café I took up
my position in hiding, and closely watched the
door. After a little Sidney came out, called a taxi
and drove away. Immediately afterwards there
emerged the man whom Sidney had described to
me, called another taxi and went in pursuit of him.
In a third cab I followed him. Sidney drove
straight back to the place where we lived, and the
spy, seeing no advantage in further pursuit, left
him there. Shortly afterwards I lost my quarry in
the traffic.

For the next two or three weeks Sidney hunted
high and low for this man. At the end of that time
my husband and I were dining in a famous New
York restaurant. Just before we sat down a friend
came up to Sidney, and they went out together. In

excusing himself to me Sidney said that he would not be away more than five minutes.

But five minutes passed and he had not come. A quarter of an hour went by, and still he was absent. At the end of half an hour I was thoroughly alarmed. I went outside and asked the doorkeeper if my husband had gone out. The doorkeeper, who knew Sidney, did not remember having seen him.

At the end of an hour I went back to our home. Sidney was not there. I will make no attempt to describe my feelings as hour followed hour and still he did not return. I did not know what to do nor what steps to take.

What had happened in the meantime was this. Sidney parted with his friend at the door of the restaurant and was just about to return to me, when who should pass but the man for whom he had been searching high and low during the last few weeks? Sidney wasted no time. Just as he was, in evening dress, without coat or hat, he went in pursuit, and this time the chase was rewarded. He followed the man to a house, where his quarry knocked in a peculiar manner. The door was half opened and the man slipped in. Sidney kept the house under observation for some time. Several other men arrived, one or two of whom he knew to be Bolsheviks, knocked in the same manner and were admitted. And in this way was discovered the great haunt of the Bolsheviks in New York.

From this place the Soviet was financing the cause of revolution in America, distributing propaganda, and incidentally trying to raise loans in America. From here too Sidney's own movements were being watched.

In a short time we had a complete list of the names and descriptions of the people from whom we might fear danger in New York. About half of them were American citizens, but there was not one who was not Russian by birth.

CHAPTER FIVE

Before me as I write I have the mass of correspondence which passed between my husband and Commander E. The Commander was an old friend of Sidney's and had served with him in the Intelligence Department during the War. He was now attached to the British Consular service at a town very close to the Russian frontier.

On a superficial reading these letters, which passed between E. in the Baltic and Sidney in New York, might seem to deal entirely with a commercial enterprise in which the correspondents were interested. Some of them indeed had no deeper significance. Others, to whosoever had eyes to see, were carrying backwards and forwards information of the gravest political and international importance.

One of these dated from Reval, January 24th, 1925, I will quote at length:

DEAR SIDNEY,

There may call on you in Paris from me two persons named Krasnoshtanov, man and wife. They will say they have a communication from California and hand you a note consisting of a verse from Omar Kahyam which you will remember. If you wish to go further into their business you must ask them to remain. *If* the business is of no interest you will say "Thank you very much, Good Day."

Now as to their business. They are representatives of a concern which will in all probability have a big influence in the future on the European and American Markets. They do not anticipate that their business will fully develop for two years, *but circumstances may arise which will give them the desired impetus in the near future.* It is a very big business and one which it does not do to talk about, as others, who have a suspicion that the concession is obtainable, would give their ears to know all about who is at the back of it and why they themselves cannot make any headway. There are especially two parties very much interested. One, a strong International group, would like to upset the whole concern as they fear their own financial interest in the event of the enterprise being brought to a satisfactory conclusion. The other, a German group, would like very much to come in, but the originators, represented by the two persons mentioned above, through whom it is important that arrangements for future communication be made, and who have worked hard on the preliminary work ever since they left Russia, will have nothing to do with them as they fear this particular group would want to take too much into their own hands. They have therefore *connected up with a smaller French group* consisting of less ambitious persons. The undertaking is so large, however, that they fear this group will not be able to handle it alone. They are therefore wanting to enter into negotiations with an English group who would be willing to work in with the French group. It is to be thoroughly understood, however, by anyone coming in that when the enterprise is firmly established the board will be composed from those who have done the spade work. *They refuse at present to disclose to anyone the name of the man at the back of this enterprise.* I can tell you this much—that some of the chief persons interested *are members of the opposition groups.* You can therefore fully understand the necessity for secrecy.

A talk with the representatives will enable you to form your own judgement as to the feasibility of their ideas.

I am introducing this scheme to you thinking it might perhaps replace the other big scheme you were working on but which fell through in such a disastrous manner. Incidentally, you would help me considerably by taking the matter up. The only thing I ask is that you keep our connection with this business from the knowledge of my department as, being a government official, I am not supposed to be connected with any such enterprise. I know your interest in such a business where patience and perseverance against all sorts of intrigues and opposition are required and I know also you will look after my interests without my having to make some special agreement with you.

Please let me know where to address letters to you in the future.

Kindest regards and best of luck. Please also remember me to your wife.

This letter calls perhaps for a little interpretation. California stands for Russia, the verse from Omar Kahyam [*sic*] for a cipher message: the big scheme which fell through disastrously was the Savinkoff affair. The letter means in fact that there is in operation a strong anti-Bolshevik group, having at its head some of the members of the Bolshevik Government.

Sidney's reply is highly interesting, as it shows his relations with the anti-Bolshevik groups and incidentally his view of their schemes, intrigues, mutual jealousies and general fatuity.

MY DEAR E.,

I was awfully pleased to receive your letter of the 26th with the extremely interesting enclosure of January 24th. I am kicking myself for not being in Paris, and thereby missing the Californian couple. You must understand that although I am here I am not losing touch with the situation at all and am in constant correspondence with the different manufacturing groups in the various countries.

I fully realise the possible importance of the scheme which the Californian Promoters have in hand. Since the failure of the big scheme on which I was working, and especially since the recent fight for share control which has been going on in the Board of Directors, I have finally convinced myself that the initiative must come direct from the present minority interests. I believe that the time is gradually getting ripe for the minority interests to realise that the whole business will go to wreck and ruin unless they make up their minds to sacrifice a good portion of their original ideas and come down to earth in a manner which will be acceptable both to the internal and international market. Whether the minority interests have already reached this mental attitude or not it has been impossible for me to discover in any definite form, and, therefore, I regret so intensely missing the Californians.

From my very intimate knowledge of the manufacturers in France, Germany and England I am convinced that the Californians will waste their time in negotiating with them. To these people the process of competition seems to be more important and vital than the achievement of mutually beneficial results. I am

casting around in my mind who of all the well-known
manufacturers is worth talking to, and I would say
that to-day probably the most practical man amongst
them, although by no means the best known or the most
popular, would be my friend Aig,[1] who at the beginning of 1917 (when the new business was organised)
held the same position which my friend of the recent
disaster held later. He has learned a lot during his
enforced retirement, is intensely energetic and is, as I
positively know, very well looked upon by the minority
interests of the Board of Directors. I have no faith
either in the manufacturers who operated under the
old patents, or in those who succeeded them and made
such a mess in working the new patents. If I was in
Paris now and the Californians came to me I would
bring them together with Aig, although I consider it
very likely that they will go to him in any case. If you
still have the possibility of getting in direct touch with
the Californians please tell them that in my opinion
negotiations with the manufacturers in Paris, London
and Berlin are a waste of time. It will be plenty of
time to bring them in when something very definite has
been decided by the minority interests. The later these
manufacturers are brought into the situation the better
it will be all round.

The minority interests are fully acquainted with the
internal market; they know exactly what is required,
and they know how and by what means the business
can be reorganised, but what they probably lack is, first
—money, and secondly—an understanding with the
leading personalities in the international market. Without such an understanding, very carefully and with
great discretion arrived at in advance, the eventual
reorganisation cannot possibly rest on a solid basis,

[1] Alexander Ivanitch Goutchkoff.

especially from a financial point of view. In these two respects all the present manufacturers put together cannot be of any help.

As regards money, the market for this kind of undertaking is here and only here, but to obtain money one must come here with a very definite and very plausible scheme, and with very substantial proof that the minority interest is able within a reasonable time to undertake and to carry out a reorganisation of the business. With such premises it would be possible to approach here in the first instance the largest automobile manufacturer,[1] who could be interested in the patents provided proof (not merely talk) was given him that the patents will work. Once his interest is gained the question of money can be considered solved.

As regards a closer understanding with the international market, I think that to start with only one man is really important, and that is the irrepressible Marlborough.[2] I have always remained on good terms with him and last year, after the disaster of my big scheme, I had a very interesting correspondence with him on the subject. His ear would always be open to something really sound, especially if it emanated from the minority interests. He said as much in one of his very private and confidential letters to me.

These are only a few of the ideas which I have on the subject of your letter of the 24th. In any case I would welcome it very much if the Californian promoters would get in touch with me, either by coming here or by correspondence. I am sure that it will be of mutual benefit, not only to the whole situation but to each of us individually.

Very sincerely yours,

[1] Henry Ford.
[2] Winston Churchill.

Dated Reval, March 9th, is a letter on an indifferent subject, but containing coded instructions for the use of a certain chemical developer. The hidden message which is revealed by the use of the developer reads as follows:

Under separate cover I am sending you a letter from Nic. Nic. Bunakoff (on yellow paper) which you can answer direct to him. His address is N. N. Bunakoff A/B Ekonomic O/V Esplanadgatan 37 Helsingfors. You can use this ink with him also, but if you do then put the initials N.N.B. somewhere on the paper, at the left hand side of the paper near the bottom. K. referred to in his letter is Koutepoff; the Schultzes are the two people who were to see you in Paris and whom I named Krashnoshtanov. When writing to N.N.B. please write him a personal letter replying to his questions or asking for any further information you may require, and another letter which he can show to the Moscow Centre or its representatives to the effect that you are interested in the commercial proposition submitted and putting forward any suggestion you may have to make and at the same time if possible give them something which will show that you are in a position to help them. This letter is not so important; what is chiefly wanted is a letter from you to N.N.B. which he can produce so that he can show that he is working on the matter.

Sidney's replies, dated respectively the 25th and 30th March, and April 4th are as follows:

25th March, 1925.

MY DEAR E.,
The letters from the Helsingfors representatives of the Syndicate are very interesting, but, as usual in

these cases, are too vague. I shall follow your advice and write to him direct. I shall write very fully and put all the dots on the i's, as in my opinion and also judging by the extremely valuable estimates which you are sending me, the situation is such that one ought at least to begin to come down to bedrock. Information and connections are of course excellent things, and I can quite appreciate their value to you especially, and, in a broader sense, to all of us. But all this does not bring us any nearer, unless the information and connections are such that they generate action.

I cannot sufficiently impress upon you how indifferent everybody has become everywhere towards this particular business. It is natural and quite comprehensible. Here is a business which for over seven years has been holding out almost daily a promise of reorganisation and payment of dividends. For years everybody was waiting with bated breath for these promises to be fulfilled and, as you know, a good many have extended considerable financial and moral credit on the strength of this expectation, but years have passed, the promises have not been realised and it is only natural that those who were interested have gone about their own business and practically given up the position as hopeless. Only *action* can arouse them out of this indifference. This action can take several forms and it is about this that I am going to write in detail to your friend.

I am not going to advocate anything rash or anything final, but in my opinion there are certain very definite things which can be done and ought to be done. One of them is a declaration by the Syndicate of its existence and of its business policy because it is primarily essential that the world at large should know that there is right on the spot a Syndicate which is capable and ready to take over the business management. This in one way or another (the form is subject

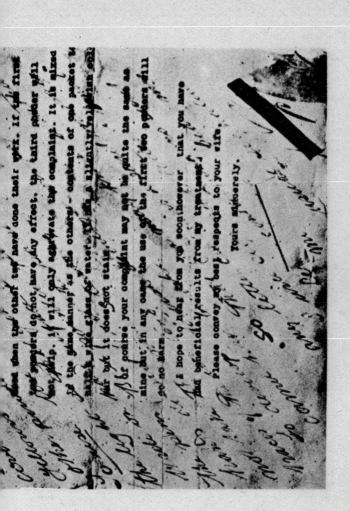

LETTER FROM COMMANDER E. TO CAPT. REILLY SHOWING SECRET WRITING
BROUGHT TO VIEW BY FOLLOWING THE TYPEWRITTEN INSTRUCTIONS

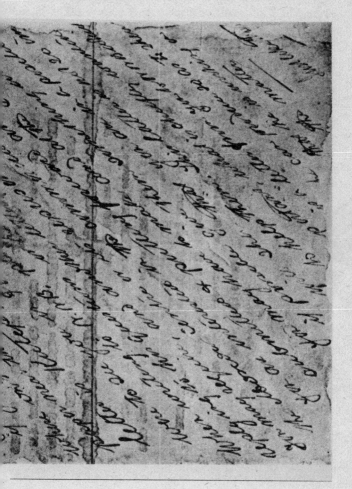

THE SECRET WRITING CONTINUED ON THE BACK OF THE PREVIOUS LETTER

to discussion) is the first step that in my opinion must be taken. I am positive that if this step is taken in the right form, it will produce a very good impression and will create everywhere an atmosphere in which it will again be possible to do useful work.

I am convinced that I shall be in a position to assist the Syndicate very materially both here and at home, and I am writing to your friend in this sense.

Much as I am concerned about my own personal affairs which, as you know, are in a hellish state, I am at any moment, if I see the right people and prospects of real action, prepared to chuck everything else and devote myself entirely to the Syndicate's interests.

I was 51 yesterday and I want to do something worth while, whilst I can. All the rest does not matter. I am quite sure that you, although younger, feel likewise.

Needless to say how deeply grateful I am to you for bringing me into this situation. I feel sure that if we are dealing with the right people, we will be able to work out something not only of the greatest interest generally, but possibly also of the greatest advantage to ourselves.

I shall write to you some more later.

Meantime ———

                              Yours ever,

P.S. Incidentally I should ask you by the next letter to give me as full a character sketch of your friend as you can.

Subject to certain transactions which I have on hand now going through, I intend, as soon as possible, to leave here for Europe, for a two-three months' trip. I would probably arrange my itinerary in such a way as to come to Reval and Helsingfors after a preliminary short stay in London. I shall let you know well in advance when I am likely to leave here.

30th March.

DEAR E.,

On second thoughts I have decided to send my letter to E. through you—both for safety and because I want you to be fully informed.—I had to write it all by hand, because I could not trust anybody to copy it. It will mean considerable trouble for you to read it, but please do so. Without wishing to be in any way arbitrary, I considered it however necessary to put the dots on the i's. I think this is the only way to come down to tintacks. I am sick and tired of this continuous theorizing. What I propose would put the organisation immediately into the forefront of the entire movement and make an end of the entirely useless emigrant factions who singly and severally are discrediting the cause everywhere.

The greatest difficulty which I see in the realisation of my scheme is the question of its representation abroad.—I cannot think of a single name which would unquestionably be accepted abroad.—

I see that at present the chief representative is Gen. K. He is a fine, active and honest man (I met him in the South in 1919) but is he not very intimately identified with the Monarchists? I surmise that the tendencies of the Central Organisation or of, at least, some of its members are towards Monarchism (otherwise why the liaison with N.N.?). Personally, I have nothing against it, *under certain circumstances and conditions,* but I would consider any *definite* association with Monarchism at the present stage as absolutely fatal as far as foreign moral and material support is concerned—I think that the representation ought to consist of three men; it would carry more weight and it will be easier to find three more or less suitable names than one ideally suitable.

If my proposals are adopted (with the necessary

modifications which may be dictated by circumstances unknown to me) and if I will be asked to participate in the execution of the scheme, I shall gladly do so and submit further details of a practical nature.

I am very anxious to hear from you your own opinion on the entire matter and especially on the proposals contained in my letter to B.

Here is another letter:

April 4th, 1925.

DEAR E.,

I received to-day copy of the Board's letter of the 15th ult. addressed to B.

In a way it is an anticipated negative answer to some of my proposals to B. enclosed in my letter of the 30th ult. to you.—I still do not agree with the Directors and I think neither do you. Apparently we were thinking pretty much on the same lines, as the Board's letter seems to be a direct reply to suggestions made by you to B. prior to your receiving my letter of the 10th of February.

On the other hand, I fully agree with the Board that the simplest and most direct way to gather all the necessary data and to arrive at a complete understanding as to future operations and improvements of manufacture is for me to come out and to inspect the factory personally.

I am not only willing but anxious to do so and am prepared to come out as soon as I have arranged my affairs here. Of course, I would undertake this tour of inspection only after very thorough consultation with you and Engineer B. Whilst there is no limit to which I am not prepared to go in order to help putting this new process on the market, I would naturally hate to provide a Roman holiday for the competitors. I think that I am not exaggerating in presuming that a successful inspection of the factory by me and the presentation of a fully substantiated technical report would produce a considerable impression in the interested quarters and generally facilitate to realisation of the scheme.

I am looking forward to your more definite advices which ought to reach me about the 20th inst. and in the meantime I shall do all to make myself free for a quick departure,—

We were now ready to leave America: my husband had accepted a position as director of a large firm in Europe, but, as his services would not be required for another month or two, we decided to spend the spare time in investigating the value of this new organisation.

On July 4th we received a telegram.

"All arrangements for general meeting made here. Waiting the date of your arrival."

To which we replied:

"Leaving finally 26th of August, Paris September 3rd."

CHAPTER SIX

Commander E. met us at Paris and we dined together on the night of our arrival. The following day I went to Ostend on a visit to my mother, whom I had not seen for over a year.

Here I received a letter from Sidney which included the following paragraph:

"I had a full day yesterday with Gen. K., G—ff, B—ff, and of course Commander E. K. impressed me very favourably. He is very 'terre à terre', has absolutely *no* illusions, depends *only* on what can be accomplished *inside*. We agreed to *lay* all cards on the table, but so far in view of the vastness of the subject we have only cleared the preliminary ground and found ourselves, I am glad to say, in complete agreement as to the theoretical appreciation of the entire situation.

"The all important questions of methods, tactics, ways and means we cannot discuss before Tuesday, as K. *must* be out of town till then. At all events it is clear that if anything at all is to be accomplished I will have to go to H—s to meet K.'s inside friends.

"G. is out of town (attending to his heart ailment) but has instructed his nephew to give me all the latest news. G. will probably have to come to Paris for a meeting with me."

After a few days I returned to Paris. Sidney told me that he was convinced of the sincerity and potentiality of this anti-Bolshevik organisation. It had been arranged that he should meet the principals of the group on the frontier between Russia and Finland, as it was decided that a journey into Russia was very dangerous. General K. was strongly of this view. The general made a very favourable impression upon me, as he had upon Sidney. We all dined together the night before we left Paris, and General K. impressed very emphatically upon my husband the folly of crossing the border.

"Let them come to you," he said. "The arrangement has been made most definitely with the people from the Moscow centre that they are to come to Helsingfors to see you there."

It was arranged that I should accompany my husband as far as Hamburg and there await his return. Except for the few days I had been at Ostend and to which I have already referred, we had not been separated for one day of our married life. But I was fain to acquiesce in the arrangement. His arrival in Helsingfors would be less noticed if he came alone than if I accompanied him. Besides as he was not going into Russia there was nothing particular for me to worry about.

The day before our departure we were leaving the Hotel Terminus, arm-in-arm, when a small dapper man suddenly dashed in front of us and took a snapshot of us. We had not time to recover from our astonishment when he jumped into a waiting taxi and was gone. The incident greatly amused us at the time, but when we told the story

to E. that night he became very alarmed and asked
all sorts of questions about the man. His alarm
communicated itself to me, and I must admit that
on the following day, the day fixed for our departure, I was feeling quite unreasonably nervous.

We were to catch the night express for Berlin,
and dined beforehand with Z. It was the first time
I had met this man, who was well known to my
husband, and I must admit at once that the impression he made on me was far from favourable. He
came to the station to see us off. My husband had
told him that we were going to Berlin, but at the
station he put some very adroit questions to me
about our journey.

"I wish you had not let this man bring us to the
station," said I to my husband.

Owing to the short notice at which our journey
had been arranged there had been no time to re-
serve seats in the sleeper, and my husband bribed
the train official to find us some good seats. Until
the train was due to start the official put us into a
reserved compartment, into which almost immediately there entered a young man. The newcomer
began at once to tell us that the compartment had
been reserved entirely for him but that he would
be honoured if we would share it with him. There
was perhaps nothing but courtesy in the remark.
What *was* strange was that he made it in Russian.
How did he know my husband spoke Russian? Or
what was he? Why should he use a language suffi-

ciently outlandish there in Paris to a stranger who was obviously an Englishman?

Again I had the sensation, with which I had become so familiar, that we were being followed. At Cologne I parted from my husband, for I was going to Hamburg to await his return there, while he was proceeding first to Berlin. It was with a very heavy heart that I stood there on the platform waiting for his train to leave. I know not wherefore, but a feeling of impending calamity was on me. I remember the surprised look on Sidney's face when, inspired by I know not what strange fear of the future, I suddenly said to him.

"Please give me E.'s address."

Sidney wrote it on the newspaper he was holding and handed it down to me.

The world goes on no matter who are taking leave. Trains will not wait for ever. An official passed down the platform. A whistle shrilled. I felt Sidney suddenly lift me into his arms. Then he set me down and stepped into the train. I saw his hand waving out of infinite blackness. A lump rose in my throat. I suddenly wanted to cry. Slowly the train gathered speed. I saw the waving hand through the tear mists rapidly receding into the distance. Then it was gone. The train had swept Sidney out of my life for ever.

I went on to Hamburg. I met some people I knew there from South America. Queer how I should remember them. One is meeting people one knows every day of one's life. But I was feeling infinitely lonely and isolated. I wanted to talk to somebody about Sidney. But I dared not. It must remain a secret—where he had gone and why.

I heard from him from Berlin.

17th Sept., 1925.

MY BELOVED DARLING (he wrote)

I have a full half an hour (waiting for O.) and can just "talk a little" with you.—It was a very sad journey without you, and most of the time I was thinking about you and wondering how you are. I am glad to feel that now you are with Chamriba and that you will not be so lonely.—Please, my little one, take care of yourself, follow the Doctor's advice, don't worry, and come back to me prettier than ever and as much rested as possible.—I shall also take great care of myself, so on that account you must not worry at all. All the rest is on the knees of the Gods.—

I arrived here about six, but was *not* met by O., who was out of town on urgent business. However I got hold of him by 'phone about 7 and he will be round in a few minutes. By the way, our travelling companion whom you disliked so much *was* a Spaniard, as I said. I guessed at his nationality from the way he wrapped himself in his rug.

I will finish now as O. may be here any minute.

God bless you, my darling little sweetheart. Be of good cheer and take care of yourself. I love you always beyond everything.

The next letter was from Helsingfors, and dated Tuesday, 22nd.

Sept., 1925.

MY SWEETHEART,

I had a very rotten trip. Sunday we had very bad weather and the little steamer did everything to make the passage very uncomfortable. I was not seasick but felt very headachey and congested. Yesterday about noon we stopped for a short while at Reval and I could gaze from the deck of the steamer upon the scene of my former exploits. Reval with all its natural and architectural beauty wears a forlorn air and I do not envy E. his life there.—It must be like living in a boarding house where the landlady had seen better days. The crowd on the trip was neither interesting nor prepossessing, mostly Germans and Finns. However, I would gladly exchange a Leviathan full of Americans for them and call it a bargain.

We arrived here very late, about 5 p.m. It was very fortunate that I had wired for a room from Paris. I got the one and only free. I got into touch with E.'s assistant (a very intelligent youngster, keen as mustard and most anxious to serve me in every possible way). He could not tell me much more than I already knew, but he attached great importance to the whole scheme and to my participation in it: then I saw Bunakoff (the man I had been in correspondence with). Although he is merely what we call a post office box, he could give me a considerable amount of useful information. B. is a very nice fellow and I am sure you would have liked him at first sight. A gentleman, unpretentious, not an eagle, though not without shrewdness and a considerable sense of humour. He enjoys the full confidence of E. and his assistant, but, as I have said, his rôle is purely secondary. He took me to his flat and gave me a wonderful Russian dinner. The piroshki were a dream, and I longed to put a couple into my pocket and bring them home to you. Mrs. Bunakoff was also a dream, but a bad one. Enormous, elephantine female with peroxidized bobbed hair, black eyebrows and eyes like hot house plums, silly as a boot, absolutely ignorant as regards politics, but otherwise harmless and of course most hospitable.

How perfectly normal and sane men get hold of *such* life companions is the greatest puzzle to me. (I must try and make a limerick on this subject.) Bunakoff and I plunged into our subject only after Mrs. B. had retired.

Very soon the two Schultzes came and the conference got into its full stride. The Schultzes (who are the link between the C. and the outer world) are a most extraordinary couple. He is just a boy, probably a very fine and undoubtedly a very brave boy, but of the type which you characterize as "nincompoop". She is the head of the concern, and her very long skirt cannot disguise the trousers which she is wearing.—She is of the American school-marm type, which, strangely enough, is not uncommon in Russia, very plain and unattractive, but full of character and personality. It was most instructive to talk to her (or rather to listen to her, because she did most of the talking). She was full of information. You will understand that I cannot give you here an account of what she said, but if only 25% of what she said is based on facts (and not on self-induced delusion, as is so often the case when the wish is the father of the will) then there is really something entirely new, powerful and worth while going on in Russia.—Anyway, when I leave here—I shall be fully and definitely "fixé là-dessus."

Now, however, comes the rub. There has been no news yet from the people we are expecting. A telegram is expected any moment and when it comes I will have to go to Wyborg (a night's journey from here) to meet them. The conference will last two days at the utmost and then away.—It is already out of the question that I should leave by the Wednesday boat. The next boat is on Saturday, which would bring me into

Stettin on Monday morning. But with bad luck, I may have to stay here (or in Wyborg) over the week-end, and get away only on Wednesday week. Until the expected telegram comes, I am completely at sea. Two things only are certain (I) that I must see these visitors and (II) that I must and want to get away as quickly as I possibly can.—The definite news about my movements I will have to send you by wire.—It will reach you earlier than this letter, which you will only get on Saturday morning.

(Here there followed divers instructions to me about my health and he concludes:)

Above all, don't worry about me. I feel perfectly well and my heart is overflowing with love for you. You are never out of my thoughts.

We love each other so completely that it is impossible that such love should not reap its full reward both in spiritual and material happiness.

God bless you, my sweet, beloved darling, and keep you safe and well until we meet.

Together with this came another letter written apparently an hour or two later.

SWEETHEART,

Just a few lines to tell you that the telegram has come, and that I am leaving to-morrow morning for Wyborg. I will be there Thursday and Friday; return here on Saturday morning and leave by the Saturday boat at 2 p.m. I shall write you whether I shall go from Stettin to Hamburg or to Berlin.

At all events on Monday the 28th I shall hold you in my arms—my beloved J.J.

I must repack my things and go to bed. I must be very early.

All my love is yours.

Almost simultaneously with these letters (on September 25th) arrived a telegram from Wyborg.

"Must remain over week-end leaving by Wednesday boat arriving Hamburg Friday wire me Hotel Andrea Wyborg well lovingly."

That was the last message I ever received direct from my dear husband, though his parting words to me I was to receive later and in circumstances which I shall presently have to narrate.

Of course I telegraphed him at the Hotel Andrea. I sent him a wire on an urgent business matter, which demanded an immediate reply. No answer. I wired again. Still no answer. On the 28th I wired the Hotel Andrea:

"Has Reilly arrived or when did he leave?"

The following morning back came the reply:

"Sidney Reilly shall arrive to-night Andrea."

On the 30th I wired again early in the morning. I do not know how far I walked that day, in the streets of Hamburg, unable to rest for one minute until the reply should arrive. It came during the afternoon.

"Reilly not arrived yesterday Andrea."

Thankfully I remembered the strange premonition which on the platform at Cologne had impelled me to ask for E.'s address. There it was, written on the newspaper which Sidney had handed to me, and I wired at once.

"No news from Sidney since twenty-fifth.

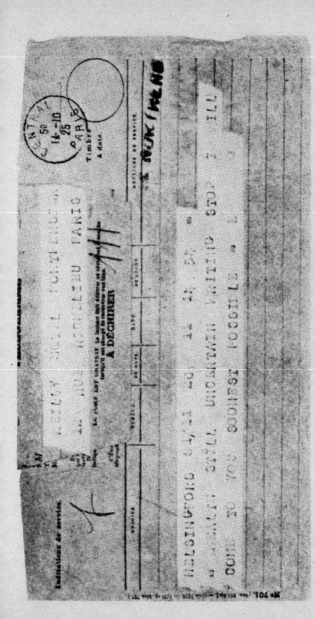

TELEGRAM FROM COMMANDER E. REPORTING TO MRS. REILLY THAT THERE IS NO NEWS OF CAPT. REILLY

Should have returned to-day. Hotel Andrea Wyborg expected him yesterday, but wired has not arrived. What steps shall I take? Wire if you have news—very anxious."

In due course came the reply from E.

"Have had no news whatever, have telegraphed."

However shall I forget the agony of those next few days? In the midst of my own family I was alone. Even to them I dared not breathe a word of Sidney's movements. What had happened to him? Surely he had not allowed himself to be lured over the border into Russia.

I remembered his own words: "Whatever you do, do not go into Russia." I remembered K.'s emphatic words on the same subject. What had happened then? Why had he not let me know? Where was he at the moment? What had happened? What *had* happened?

Several days passed before I received a letter from Commander E.

October 1st.

Dear Mrs. Reilly (it ran)

I have heard from no one as to Sidney's condition. In fact I have had no news from that part of the world since I left.

Judging from your telegram he has apparently undergone the operation after all. This is rather a surprise to me as I thought the doctors in Paris considered it unnecessary. I suppose further complications must have set in which decided him to have the operation. As I understood it the operation was a simple one but his recovery might take a little longer than was expected. We must not get panicky. I am sure he is in safe hands and everything will be done to make his recovery as speedy as possible. It will not help us to send frantic telegrams. We shall hear as soon as he is able to get about again.

On the heels of this letter came another bearing the same date.

DEAR MRS. REILLY,

Since writing I have received a postcard dated the 27th September which indicates that he was all right then, and it is unlikely that sufficient time could have elapsed by the 29th for him to have completely recovered from the operation, so there is nothing to worry about yet.

The following day came another letter from Commander E., announcing that he had now definitely the information that complications had set in, i.e. that Sidney had gone to Russia.

5th October.

MY DEAR JEFF[1]

I certainly think that it will be a very good idea to consult the Paris Surgeon. Unfortunately I have forgotten his name but I know it began with a K. I have asked a friend of mine by letter to let him know your address and to call on you.

It is a very sad thing about poor old Mutt. I do hope he pulls through all right. You know he was very fond of you, and before going into the hospital he left a letter for you with instructions that it should be sent on if he was incapable of writing himself after the operation. This letter is now being sent on to Paris to

[1] Jeff is myself, and Mutt Sidney.

you. The doctors have asked that no further enquiries
be made about him as it only harasses them. They will
report any change in his condition. He has a strong
constitution and should pull through, but it will be very
slow. He is well looked after and everything possible
is being done for him. He will not want for necessities
when he recovers, but you will soon be informed how
and where to send any money you may wish. I have had
no further telegram and so suppose things are taking
their normal course.

And so I returned to Paris. What a different
Paris it was from the place I had left! The sun
was shining brightly, but all his beams brought me
no light. Everywhere were people laughing, talking, joking, faring about their business. The traffic
roared in the streets. The evening came and the
theatres opened at the usual time, as if—as if Sidney had not disappeared to an unknown fate and
my heart been shattered to atoms a few short hours
before.

I went to the Hotel Terminus, Gare St. Lazare,
where we had stayed together, where our trunks
rested even now. I was alone, and all the rest of
the world infinitely removed from me. I had done
with it all for evermore. It was my ghost that had
returned to visit the place where a short time before I had been so happy.

In the lounge a man stared at me with a sort of
triumphant smile. I remembered the face somewhere. But I was past caring. Only when he had
gone memory flashed back on me. It was Drebkoff.

General K. called to see me. But he had no news.

He could speak only Russian. He was very kind, very consoling, but—of what use was it all, of what use was life, of what use was anything?

A letter arrived from Commander E., dated from Helsingfors, October 11th.

MY DEAR JEFF,

As I found it impossible to get anything definite out of my friends I finally decided to proceed to the place and see if I could find out anything more definite for you.

As you know the business was of such importance that it was considered necessary to keep it as secret as possible, and this secrecy is making it difficult to get at the facts.

It would appear that everything went according to programme (I am talking now of the new plans) until the very last moment when one of those unfortunate coincidences occurred, which had apparently no direct bearing on this particular business, but which, unexpectedly entering into the case, completely upset all the plans and left the parties concerned in a most parlous condition. Every precaution was taken and every circumstance which could be thought of arranged for, but quite unwittingly they fell across an influence which was working on different lines at the very last moment and this has brought ruin on all three of the negotiators. Whether they will be able to extricate themselves finally and restart their negotiations is at present an unknown quantity. I am awaiting the arrival of a special report from the place which they intended to make the centre of their activities, but this as you will imagine may take some time. They have carried on their negotiations with such secrecy that it is very difficult, in fact almost impossible, for them to get anyone outside their own circle to help them, and further this opposing influence, not having realised the significance of what they have done, cannot be informed as to the real object of your business friends as that would ruin the one and only chance of their being able to reconstruct their affairs and get out of the present impasse.

Not being in their confidence, I am in the very unfortunate position of being only an outsider and therefore unable to bring any influence to bear on the subject. By insisting on being allowed to participate I should only work against your interests.

In the meantime I have been able to assure myself that all papers and documents have been kept intact. Any papers you may have bearing on this subject please keep in a very safe place as there is no knowing what may happen and it is very important that no inkling of what the scheme was should fall into the hands of the opposing parties.

Stockholm,
October 18th.

DEAR JEFF,

I am on my way to Paris via London and hope to be with you on Thursday or latest Friday.

The position I am sorry to say is much worse than I had hoped from the information previously received. It appears that at the last moment just before they hoped to complete the whole business a party of four of them were prospecting in the forests near by and were suddenly attacked by brigands. They put up a fight with the result that two were killed outright. Mutt was seriously wounded and the fourth taken captive.

Further information as to the whereabouts and conditions of the captives is difficult to get. Two parties were sent out to investigate. One, which went to the place of the fight, returned and confirmed the facts as given above. The second had not returned yet, but is expected daily. I hope by time I get to Paris to have some news of them.

It is not known yet whether this attack by the brigands was organised in connection with the business Mutt was engaged on, but it is thought that it was not, but was purely an unexpected occurrence having no direct bearing on the matter. It is none the less very disturbing as I very much fear, from the accounts brought back by the first party, that Mutt's injuries were very serious. I sincerely hope that the other party will bring back more reassuring news.

When we meet we shall have to discuss the question of what future action is to be taken.

But I did not see Commander E. in Paris after all. On the 23rd I received a letter from him dated from London, which read as follows:

My dear Jeff,

I have had no later information and do not now see how I can get any as my only possible source, I hear, has left Helsingfors and is now on his way to Paris to see you. You will therefore be advised earlier than I shall. I don't know when I shall hear any more about it as I find urgent business now which takes me abroad again immediately and prevents me coming to Paris.

Furthermore I shall have no permanent address for some time, but will let you know later where I am to be found if you will give instructions for letters to be forwarded from your present address. *Au revoir* and trusting you will soon get more definite and satisfactory information.

And so the last straw at which I was clutching in my agony had swam out of my reach. The one Englishman who had appeared in the whole transaction, the only person whom I felt that I could trust, had run away and left me. The people in whose hands I was left were strangers of a race which I had grown to loathe and fear. Any or all of them might be Bolshevik agents. I knew none of them. All I knew was that the Tcheka had thrown its net successfully at last, and Sidney had been cozened by the provocation agents, who had lured D. from London, Savinkoff from Paris, Mme. Schovalovsky from New York.

Yes, it was all quite clear, and these people, in whose hands Commander E. had left me, to whose tender mercies my future hopes were consigned, were for all I knew agents of the Red Terror. Nay, I thought, why should Commander E. himself not be in the pay of the Tcheka?

Bunakoff arrived in Paris at last. He spoke nothing but Russian, but he handed over to me the letter, which, for reasons best known to himself, he had retained till now.

It was dated from Wyborg, September 25th, the very day on which Sidney had sent me his last telegram, and this is how it ran:

My most beloved, my sweetheart,

It is absolutely necessary that I should go for three days to Petrograd and Moscow. I am leaving to-night and will be back here on Tuesday morning. I want you to know that I would not have undertaken this trip unless it was absolutely essential, and if I was not convinced that there is practically no risk attached to it. I am writing this letter only for the most improbable case of a mishap befalling me. Should this

Wyborg 25th Sept. 1925
Friday.

My most beloved, my sweetheart,
. It is absolutely necessary that
I should go for three days to
Petrograd and Moscow. I am
leaving tonight and will be back
here on Tuesday morning. I want
you to know that I would not
have undertaken this trip unless
it was absolutely essential and
if I was not convinced that
there is practically no risk attached
to it. — I am writing this letter
only for the most unprobable case
of a mischance befalling me.
Should this happen, then you
must not take any steps. They
will help little but

CAPT. REILLY'S LAST LETTER TO MRS. REILLY

may finally lead to giving the
alarm to the Bolshies and to
disclosing my identity. If by any
chance. I should be arrested in
Russia, it could only be on some
minor. insignificant charge
and my new friends are powerful
enough to obtain my prompt.
liberation. I cannot imagine
any circumstances under which
the Bolshies could tumble to
my identity — provided nothing
is done from your side. —
Therefore, if I should have
some trouble, it would only —
mean a very short delay in
my return to Europe. I should
say a fortnight at the most.

Knowing you, I am certain
that you will rise to the occasion

Keep your head and do all
that is necessary to keep the fort
as regards my business affairs.

Naturally, none of these people
must get an inkling where
I am and what has happened
to me. — Remember, that
every noise etc. may give
me away to the Bolshies.

My dearest darling, I am
doing what I must do and
I am doing it with the absolute
inner assurance that if you
were with me, you would approve.

You are in my thoughts
always and your love will
protect me. God bless you ever
and ever. I love you beyond
all words.   Sidworth Ra...

happen, then you must not take any steps; they will help little but may finally lead to giving the alarm to the Bolshies and to disclosing my identity. If by any chance I should be arrested in Russia, it could be only on some minor, insignificant charge and my new friends are powerful enough to obtain my prompt liberation. I cannot imagine any circumstance under which the Bolshies could tumble to my identity provided nothing is done from your side. Therefore, if I should have some trouble, it would only mean a very short delay in my return to Europe—I should say a fortnight at the most. Knowing you I am certain you will rise to the occasion, keep your head, and do all that is necessary to keep the fort as regards my business affairs.

Naturally none of these people must get an inkling where I am and what has happened to me, and remember that every noise, etc., may give me away to the Bolshies.

My dearest darling, I am doing what I must do and I am doing it with the absolute inner assurance that, if you were with me, you would approve. You are in my thoughts always and your love will protect me. God bless you ever and ever. I love you beyond all words.

That was all. There it was in his beloved handwriting. This had come back in the place of the man I had lost. I read the words through a mist of tears. The autumn sun sinking to his setting lit up the room with beams of lurid red. And somewhere far away my husband had met a fate which no man knew at the hands of his implacable enemies. The Tcheka had lured Sidney Reilly back to Russia at last.

Part Three

MRS. REILLY'S NARRATIVE

(Continued)

CHAPTER ONE

"He's gone-gone-gone," said the train speeding towards Dieppe, "and he's gone-gone-gone."

The passenger opposite was asleep, his face supported on his hand. Through the window the grey landscape unwound and hurried into the past. I now had no fear that I was followed. The Tcheka had achieved its purpose, and its agents had melted into the shadows from which they had come. And I was going to London—to find Sidney.

It was terrible—doing nothing in Paris. I felt like a lost wanderer in the crowd of life. I could not remain. My Russian acquaintances there—I had no friends—were dumbly sympathetic. They were helpless. They could do nothing. What was to be done? They had spent years waiting in the ante-chamber of Fortune. They were fatalists. They were content to wait. They were sorry, very sorry, but—— They had lives, cares, worries of their own. They were strangers to me. Who could help me? Z. could not. General K. could not. There was Commander E. And Commander E. had gone abroad. He would be "away some time". There was no one to help. And I knew nothing. I was ignorant. It was as if the world had combined in a conspiracy against me—against me and Sid-

ney. I remembered how at dinner in Paris, before
Sidney had set forth upon that fatal journey, Commander E. had mentioned, in the course of conversation, that when in London he usually stayed
at the —— Street Hotel. If he had not yet gone
abroad, he would be there now. It was a poor
chance, but one who drowns proverbially clutches
at a straw. I *might* catch him there. Something I
must do. I could not wait. I could not sit still and
do nothing. And so I set forth from Paris on my
wild-goose chase—for London and the Hotel.

I had no suspicions now of my fellow travellers.
I was past fearing. I did not think that I was
watched. The thought gave me no pleasure, only
another stab of anguish every time that my mind
recurred to it, and I remembered—each time with
a new and entirely fresh realisation—that the
Tcheka's work was done, and he was gone, for
whom they had watched and waited.

The crowd at the Gare du Nord was indifferent.
People were seeing off friends, relations, dear ones.
For me, the tide of life had passed over my head
and engulfed me.

I arrived late in London. I called a cab and
drove to the Hotel. A feeling almost of suffocation
came over me as I approached it. Had I come on
a wild-goose chase after all? Would I find Commander E. there? Had he already departed on the
journey of which he had spoken in his last letter?

I arrived at the hotel and booked a room for the

night. I was tired out. I asked to be shown immediately to my room.

"By the way," I asked the porter as I followed
him across the foyer, "is Commander E. staying
here?"

"Yes, madam," he replied. My heart gave a
little bound, but I veiled my excitement with a
yawn.

"It doesn't matter," I said with an affected carelessness of manner. "I will see him in the morning
perhaps. At what time does he take breakfast?"

"About nine o'clock, madam," replied the
porter.

So the first part of my mission was successfully
accomplished. I was determined. Come what
might I was going to find out what had happened
to Sidney. I was going to him—even if I had to
go to Russia to find him—I was going to him.
Nothing should stop me. I would find him.

Next morning I waited until E. had finished his
breakfast before I revealed myself to him. For
my part I was too disturbed to eat anything. As
he came out of the room I emerged from the recess
in which I had concealed myself and called him
by name. To say that Commander E. was surprised to see me but faintly describes the stress of
emotion under which he suffered at that moment.

"You," he gasped. "You?"

"Where can we talk in peace and quietness?"
I asked him.

Without a word he turned and led me to a seat. His hand was trembling like a leaf.

My arrival had obviously disconcerted Commander E., but he was quite ready with an explanation of his conduct in having sought to avoid me. In the circumstances of Sidney's death, it was impolitic for a British official to be seen in my company, and he had received an instruction to that effect from his superiors. The explanation was satisfactory. Sidney himself had repeatedly told me that "the service must not be brought into it."

I talked with E. for some time. He could add nothing to what I already knew. The party of men, with which Sidney was, had been attacked by bandits as it returned to the frontier. Sidney had been badly wounded. What his ultimate fate was E. did not know, but he feared the worst.

"But we have our agents in Russia," he assured me. "They will find out in time, you may be certain of that."

There was obviously no help here. But I had another string to my bow. There was the Foreign Office. I had written to Captain Hill, telling him of my news. He came at once to my help. But the Foreign Office either could or would do nothing. The papers were strangely silent. Not a word had escaped from the Bolsheviks of the fate of Sidney Reilly.

What to do? I was like a caged lion. I could not rest. The precious time was slipping by. The suspense was terrible—waiting, waiting. I must move. Nobody could help me. I must act for myself.

Then somewhat to my surprise, Commander E. invited me to dine with him and to meet a friend. As soon as he saw me the Commander reminded me that I had in my keeping many confidential documents, including letters from himself. As these papers would be of the utmost value to the Bolsheviks, I would be in the gravest personal danger if they remained in my keeping, and Commander E. suggested that I should hand them over to him for safe custody. This, however, I flatly refused to do. The friend whom I was to meet, turned out to be Bunakoff, who had arrived in London on a mission to Commander E. The Commander had described him as "a man who does not ask money for his services, but does not refuse money if offered"; a sufficiently apt description. I saw Bunakoff and questioned him, Commander E. acting as interpreter. Bunakoff knew nothing. He had acted but as an intermediary for higher powers. Marie Schultz was his immediate superior. Who was Marie Schultz? That he could not say. He knew that she was in close touch with a world-wide anti-Bolshevik organisation, of which the headquarters were in Moscow itself. Beyond that—nothing. Could I see Marie Schultz? Bunakoff shrugged his shoulders. She was in Helsingfors.

During the past few days of vain labour and grief a plan had been slowly forming in my mind.

I must go to Helsingfors. Helsingfors had been
Sidney's base of operations. Helsingfors had been
the site of the "factory." In Helsingfors was Marie
Schultz. Yes, I must go to Helsingfors. There
could henceforth be no rest for me until I had
found something definite, till I could be assured
whether Sidney was dead or alive. Henceforward
I was enrolled in the anti-Bolshevik cause as an
active agent. There should be no rest for me in
the fight against that enormity, against which Sidney had fought until it had swallowed him. To
Helsingfors, then. And then? Over the border into
Russia, if need be—to Petrograd, to Moscow itself
—to find out. I knew no fear. My sorrow—my rage
against the Bolsheviks was too great for that.

Such were the thoughts which swarmed in my
mind as I dined with Bunakoff and Commander E.

I booked my passage to Helsingfors on the Hull
steamer *Astraea*. There were several days to wait.
I put my affairs in order, made a will, left final
instructions in case I did not return. Then suddenly the desire came to me to put the whole matter to somebody absolutely independent. My mind
went to Dr. Harold Williams, of *The Times*, a
man who knew Russia and had been acquainted
with my husband. To Dr. Williams I went and
told him the whole story, and that I counted on
him to take the matter up if I did not return. He
was absolutely dumbfounded when he heard the
story. At first he earnestly tried to keep me from
going to Finland, but when he saw it was useless

he promised to do all he could. Further I arranged for him to publish the announcement of my husband's death, should I wire him to do so. I had to make this arrangement as Sidney was expected back in New York on urgent business and, though I had kept the fort until now, I could not do so much longer.

It was a foggy morning when I got in the train for Hull. I boarded the *Astraea* that night. Such a queer little ship. Such a queer little cabin. Such a dear old captain. Such excellent food. Hardly ever have I tasted the like.

A telegram was waiting for me: "Good luck to a plucky brick. Hill."

I was on the captain's bridge most of the time. He looked after me like a father. He took it upon himself to be perturbed when he found that I was going to Helsingfors alone without knowing a word of the language. When he heard that friends were meeting me, he became happier. He said that he would hand me over to them himself.

It was bitterly cold, but I think that the sharp frosty wind, blowing across the bows of the *Astraea*, cleared my fevered mind and helped me to see things in a better perspective. The weather was fine. Never have I seen such stars. The nights were like day.

On our arrival at Copenhagen the captain took me to see the town and buy provisions. Next morning we were nearing Helsingfors. This was the first time I had been in this part of the world, and never, I thought, had I seen such a pretty picture as the entrance to Helsingfors harbour. It had been snowing in the night, but now there was brilliant sunshine. The place looked so small, so quaint, so white, so golden, that it seemed to me for all the world like one of those old-fashioned German Christmas cards, in which the little spire of the little church and all the little houses stand out against the white landscape.

Helsingfors! I woke from the dream. I was back to earth and stark reality. On the quay three men were awaiting me. I recognised Bunakoff at once and waved to him. The dear old captain bade me good-bye, and I left the friendly little ship.

One of the two men with Bunakoff turned out to be his brother. The other, an insignificant look-ing boy, was Schultz. I could almost recognise him from my husband's picture—"perhaps a very fine boy and undoubtedly a very brave boy, but what you would call a nincompoop."

The air was very shrewd. My hands were so cold that I could not open my trunks for the Cus-toms, and my legs were almost frozen, though I was wearing thick woollen stockings.

At last we got into a motor-car and drove through streets white with snow. Bunakoff had en-gaged me a room in a *pension*, because, as he ex-plained, the best hotel was known to be a meeting-ground of all the Bolsheviks. Helsingfors was a hot-bed of intrigue. Measure and counter-measure were being taken there, plot and counter-plot pro-

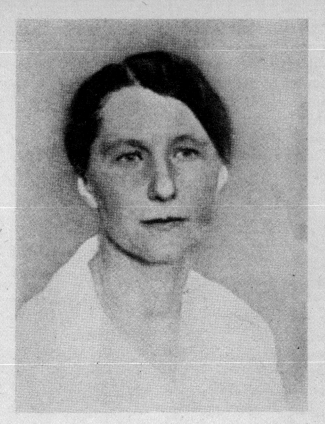

Marie Schultz

ceeded daily. It was important that I should be un-observed.

I had no complaints to make about my *pension*. It was spick and span and very clean. The bed looked very comfortable. The appointments were first class. The room had double windows and was very warm. To this day I laugh when I recall the chambermaid's cry of alarm when she brought my coffee in the morning and found that I had slept with my window open.

And here I was. The man-boy Schultz told me in broken German that his wife would call on me in one hour's time, and I was left alone. And how alone I felt God only knows. My courage seemed to have ebbed away. For the first time I felt like breaking down.

But after a good meal I began to feel more mistress of myself, and I awaited the coming of Marie Schultz with the greatest curiosity to see the woman on whom so much depended. I was naturally highly suspicious, and in my own mind had very little doubt but that she was a provocation agent.

Punctually at the hour there was a knock at the door, and in came a slender woman with plain yet attractive, capable face, steady, honest, blue eyes, obviously well bred, and answering very well to Sidney's description of her as a school ma'rm. At my first glance I decided that I could trust her. At my second I knew that I was going to like this woman.

Seeing me thus, looking very mournful, very desolate, very lonely, Mme. Schultz embraced me with great emotion, telling me that she felt herself entirely responsible for my husband's death, and that she would not rest until all the circumstances had been discovered and a rescue effected if he were still alive, or a revenge secured if he were in truth dead.

"When your husband arrived here," she told me, "I explained to him the exact situation of affairs as far as our organisation was concerned. On our side we have some of the principal Bolshevik officials in Moscow, who are anxious to bring the present *régime* to an end, if only their safety can be guaranteed. This means support from outside Russia, and it was on this point that we wanted your husband's advice. I may mention that I am in very close touch with the Moscow heads of this organisation. In fact I live in Moscow, and came here to see Captain Reilly and discuss the chances of outside help with him.

"Captain Reilly was rather sceptical. He said that foreign help could only be obtained if the nation giving it could be assured that the anti-Bolshevik organisation in Russia was more than a shadow. Granted that there was a solid body of support in Russia itself, he thought that the anti-Bolshevik *coup d'état* could be played without difficulty. But convincing proof would be required before the necessary support could be obtained.

"I assured him that our organisation in Russia

was powerful, influential and well-knit, and that it included among its members one or two highly-placed Bolshevik officials. And finally I sent a message by an agent to Moscow requesting one of the heads of the organisation to attend.

"The meeting place was fixed at Wyborg, which is much nearer the Russian frontier than Helsingfors. Our man from Russia could not venture very far over the border without arousing suspicions. Besides, there are so many Bolshevik agents here that he was bound to be recognised. Near Wyborg is living a Russian exile, who belongs to our organisation, and at his house the meeting was to take place.

"Well, we all went to Wyborg, George, Mr. Bunakoff, your husband and myself, and at the house we met the men who had come out of Russia. Your husband questioned them very searchingly, and they confirmed my words with regard to the strength of the organisation. Captain Reilly was much impressed by them, particularly by their leader, a very highly-placed Bolshevik official, who beneath the cover of his office is one of the most ardent enemies of the present *régime*. This man said that he thought it wise for your husband to meet the other heads of the organisation in order to assure himself of the importance of the movement. With this he pulled out of his pocket a passport made out in the name of Nicholas Nicholaievitch Steinberg, and invited your husband to accompany him to Moscow to verify the truth of his assertions. At the same time he assured him that the organisation was so powerful, and included such influential persons among its members, that there was absolutely no risk in his crossing the border. The "Trust", as we call ourselves, could pull him out of any difficulty. Now Captain Reilly was a very shrewd judge of character and, while the other was talking, I could see your husband eyeing him up and down, summing him up and slowly arriving at a favourable conclusion.

"The upshot of it was that he decided to make this journey to Moscow. He borrowed a suit from my husband, but wore his own linen, which was marked, his watch, which bore his initials, and a photograph of you. I mention this to show that the Bolsheviks would have no difficulty in identifying him, if they caught him.

"So the next day we set out for the frontier. We had already arranged with the Finnish patrols to see our party over the river, and I told George to accompany them as far as the train. For my part I went as far as the frontier to wish them God-speed.

"Now you must know that the frontier between Russia and Finland is marked by a narrow stream. On each side at intervals are the block-houses of the patrols, the Finnish on this side and the Russian on that. The greatest hostility exists between them, and the only communications between the one bank and the other are carried out surreptitiously and under cover of darkness. The country on each side is very sparsely populated, and you may go for miles without meeting a soul. It is necessary for our people to be ferried across this stream when the Red patrols are not looking, and then slink under cover of darkness across the open country to the railway station. They get shelter from our sympathisers among the villagers on the other side of the river.

"Well, we duly arrived at the Finnish blockhouse, Captain Reilly, George, myself and the men out of Russia. Three Finnish soldiers were there. They had reconnoitred the river bank and found all clear. They provided us with food, and we sat down and waited for night.

"The night was ideal for the venture, fine and clear. We waited for the setting of the moon and then moved off in Indian file to the river. At last our guide called a halt, and peering through the darkness we could see the rising ground the other side of the border, and its bare edge resting opaque against the deep grey of the sky. At our feet the river flowed sluggishly.

"For a long time we waited while the Finns listened anxiously for the Red patrol, but everything was quiet. At last one of the Finns lowered himself cautiously into the water and half swam, half waded across. Your husband followed. Then went one of the men out of Russia, until all were across.

"Two Finns and myself remained on this side. Peering over the water we could distinctly see them filing obliquely across the field on the further bank. Then they vanished into the gloom. By-and-by we saw their figures faintly outlined one by one against the sky as they crossed the crest. We gave them ten minutes. All was as silent as the grave, and we returned to the blockhouse.

"George returned the following day with the news that they had boarded the train without incident. All had gone well.

"Well, your husband visited Petrograd and Moscow, whence he sent postcards to yourself and Commander E. On the day appointed for his return I was at Wyborg waiting for him. But he did not arrive."

Here Mme. Schultz laid before me a cutting out of the Bolshevik paper, *Isvestia*, which ran as follows:

"The night of September 28th-29th, four contrabandists tried to pass the Finnish frontier with the result that two were killed, one a Finnish soldier, taken prisoner, and the fourth so badly wounded that he died on the way to Petrograd."

"This was the first news I had of the disaster," Mme. Schultz resumed, "and I at once sent George across the frontier to confirm the news. He questioned the peasants and they confirmed the story just as the Bolsheviks had told it. They had heard the shooting on the frontier on the night when the party should have returned."

"And do you think that my husband is dead?" I asked her.

"Who can doubt it?" she answered sadly. "According to accounts it was he who died on the journey back to Petrograd. But you are not convinced? Why should you think that he is still alive?"

"For these reasons," I told her. "If he were dead, there is no doubt that the body would have been examined: the Bolshevik police would have noticed that the man wore shirts and underwear marked S.R. They would find the watch and my photograph with an inscription in English. And they would find a passport with the name of Steinberg. Then you must remember that the Bolsheviks have in their possession several very good photographs of my husband, and there are plenty of people in Russia who know him perfectly well by sight, and me too. How then can they fail to have identified him? And if they had identified him, why have they simply put in the paper this small notice instead of shouting from the housetops that they had captured the famous Sidney Reilly like a rat? They would have been quite justified in exulting, as Sidney has twice been condemned to death *in contumaciam*. Why this silence, if he is really dead? Is it not much more likely that he has been badly wounded, but that there is still hope of his recovery, and they are only waiting for that to make a further diabolic move?"

Mme. Schultz could not but admit the force of my reasoning, and admitted that the possibility which I indicated had not previously occurred to her.

We now decided to work together on this hypothesis and endeavour to get at the truth. But where were we to begin?

Turning the matter over in my mind hour after hour that night, I suddenly remembered Sidney's Berlin acquaintance, Orloff, and I hit on an expedient of getting information from Orloff without betraying Sidney's whereabouts to him.

I wrote him a letter, which purported to be dictated to me by my husband, who was ill and could not write himself. In this I said that a very good friend of his, named Nicholas Nicholaievitch Steinberg, had met with an accident in Russia, and I should be obliged if Orloff could find out anything definite for me about him.

Orloff telegraphed his answer—to go to such-and-such address, where I could see a friend of his, to whom he had wired the story. The address was in a small street, on the first floor of a house there, and I was to ask for Nicholas Karlovitch.

So off we went, the two Schultzes and myself to the house indicated. The arrangement was that, if I did not come out in half an hour, they were to come and enquire for me. My heart was beating very fast as I went up to the door and rang the bell.

The door was opened by a short, thick-set man, whom I asked whether I could see Nicholas Karlovitch. The man bowed and smiled, asked me in and gave me a chair. I explained my mission fully. After I had finished he asked me to wait a minute, and called up a number on the telephone. I tried hard to memorise it, but it was in Finnish, which does not fall within the range of my accomplishments. After a few words with somebody at the other end of the wire, the thick-set man handed me the telephone and said that Nicholas Karlovitch would speak to me.

"But you pretended to be Nicholas Karlovitch," I said indignantly. The thick-set man smiled and shrugged.

In the meantime a suave voice was coming over the wire. It told me that its owner was very pleased I had called, and that he would give himself the honour of calling on me at my *pension* that night, if it were convenient to me. I answered that I would be delighted to see him and was proceeding to give him my address.

"Do not trouble, do not trouble," said the voice with a chuckle. "I know perfectly well where you are staying. I know the floor you are on, the room you occupy, and what you had for breakfast this morning. I will be with you at 8 o'clock to-night then."

I came away with a chill feeling at the base of my spine. I had purposely kept my address a close secret and all my letters came Poste Restante, and yet this terrible man knew all about me. The Schultzes looked grave when I told them. They at once suspected Nicholas Karlovitch of being a

Bolshevik agent, and they decided to post themselves where they could watch him when he came to see me, and follow him to see who he was and where he went.

Eight o'clock came and Nicholas Karlovitch had not arrived. At half past he rang me on the 'phone and told me he could not come until nine. I knew that the Schultzes were waiting in the bitter cold outside, but I dared not communicate with them for fear of bringing them under observation. And this was not all. They expected my visitor at eight and might follow the wrong man.

However, at nine o'clock a knock came at my door, and there stood a tall man of military build and appearance, who clicked his heels and introduced himself as Nicholas Karlovitch in the German way. When he had seated himself he told me that he had received a letter from his friend Orloff in Berlin, which left him rather in the dark, and he would be much obliged if I would explain the matter more fully.

I did so in a few words, telling him the same story as I had told Orloff but adding that my husband was ill in Paris and had sent me to enquire into the fate of his friend Steinberg.

Nicholas Karlovitch listened to my story without looking at me and without a word. But when I had finished he suddenly leaped to his feet and stared into my eyes in a dreadful, piercing, hypnotic way. His eyes were like steel gimlets and seemed to pierce to the inmost depths of my soul.

My heart turned to water and my knees became
loose beneath me; my blood seemed to freeze in
my veins; I felt as if I were paralysed. This then
was the famous Tcheka look of which I had heard
so much.

"Do you know General K.?" asked Nicholas
Karlovitch.

It was the most terrible and pregnant question
he could ask. It was understood that General K.'s
name was never to be mentioned, as his connection
with this business was supposed to be unknown
save to very few, and never did Commander E. or
my husband pronounce those fateful syllables.

With an effort I controlled myself, and answered with an air of simple unconcern:

"No, I don't know him. I think I have heard his
name. Isn't he a Russian? It's a Russian name."

"Do you think," resumed the inquisitor, never
for a moment taking his dreadful gaze off my
eyes, "that you are quite sure that you do not know
him?"

"Might he help us?" I asked innocently. "Is
he in Finland?"

The dreadful eyes held mine, and without answering my questions, Nicholas Karlovitch asked
again:

"You are quite sure you do not know him?"

My voice failed me. My tongue stuck. I shook
my head. Nicholas Karlovitch looked down.

"I think," he said, "that I might be able to help

you trace your friend, Steinberg, but, of course, it will cost money."

"I am prepared to pay for the information," I answered.

"Well, then," said Nicholas Karlovitch, "I have a friend in the Tcheka in Russia, who will be able to help you. If this Steinberg is alive, I will find out for you where he is. If he is dead, I will try and get you a photograph of the body. I will come and see you again to-morrow at the same time, and let you know how much it will cost."

A few minutes after Nicholas Karlovitch had gone, I dressed and left for the Schultzes' house. As I descended the stairs of the *pension* I passed a man on the landing. Outside the door was another. I saw Mme. Schultz in a doorway opposite but made no sign, as I realised that I was watched. At the corner of the street I took a taxicab, and the man took another.

I ordered the driver to go to the station, and arrived there just as the pursuing cab came round the corner. I went in at the door and took shelter behind a kiosk, and my pursuer running into the the station almost brushed me where I stood. As soon as he was past I slipped out of the door and jumped into a taxicab, giving the driver an address which I knew to be near the Schultzes' house. The streets were quite deserted when we arrived, and, making sure that I was not followed I entered the Schultzes' house.

Mme. Schultz was waiting for me, and lost no

time in telling me what she had observed from her vantage point. Two men had been watching in front of my house at eight o'clock. Another man shortly came by and whispered something to the watchers as he passed. On this they disappeared and returned again at about twenty minutes to nine. The Schultzes had seen the arrival of Nicholas Karlovitch at nine o'clock, and had seen him enter after being saluted by the two men. M. Schultz and another man had followed him when he left, but had not yet returned.

While we were talking together M. Schultz and his friend arrived rather dispirited. They had to own that Nicholas Karlovitch had given them the slip.

The next day I noticed that a new lodger had taken the room opposite mine. The maid, too, a stupid Finnish woman, on whom no words of mine seemed to make any impression, took to entering my room suddenly and without any pretext. When I was going out that morning, I saw her run suddenly to the back of the house and begin violently shaking a small carpet out of the window. As I passed down the stairs I took a casual glance out of one of the windows which commanded the back of the house. Two men were waiting there.

I was obviously being closely watched, and the Finnish servant had apparently signalled the news that I was going out. Sure enough I was followed from the door of the *pension*, and I amused myself by taking my trackers on a long circuitous walk.

Gnädige Frau!

Tut mir sehr leid und bitte tausendmal um Verzeihung, dass ich heute bei Ihnen Gnicht sein kann. Eine sehr wichtige Sache ist dazwischen gekommen.

Einige Neuheiten habe ich schon, aber die werde ich später mitteilen.

Wenn Sie gestatten, werde ich Ihnen morgen um 3 Uhr telefonieren.

Ihr ergeb.
Nik. Karl—tch

GRACIOUS LADY,

I am very sorry and apologise a thousand times for the fact that I cannot be with you to-day. Something very important has intervened.

I have obtained already a little information, but I will tell you about that later. If you will allow me to do so, I will telephone you at 3 o'clock to-morrow.

Yrs.,
NIK K. ITCH.

However, I expected Mme. Schultz in the course of the afternoon, and the attentions of the two men were becoming something of a nuisance. I discussed the matter with Mme. Schultz that afternoon. I was rather amused than anything else, but this constant watching was an annoyance. As we were talking the matter over and wondering how to get to the bottom of the affair, there came a frantic message from Bunakoff asking what was Mrs. Reilly doing, as he had just heard from some-body who was in his pay in the secret police that she was to be arrested.

This, of course, did not suit our plans at all, and Mme. Schultz sent her husband to the Chief of Staff of the Finnish Army. The Chief of Staff was a friend and a coadjutor of the organisation, and helped its members to cross the frontier on their various enterprises. Of course he knew all about my husband, and indeed was personally concerned in helping him over the border. M. Schultz then saw this man, explained the position to him and gave him the address which Nicholas Karlovitch had given me. M. Schultz returned with the news that the Chief of Staff was looking into the matter, and we awaited the result rather breathlessly.

That day my room was searched during my absence. But as I had the day before given into Mme. Schultz' keeping my revolver and various papers and addresses, nothing was found. And when the evening came I sat down and waited for Nicholas Karlovitch to come as he had promised and let me know the price of the investigation he was making.

Instead of Nicholas Karlovitch there came the following letter:

GNÄDIGE FRAU,

Tut mir sehr leid und bitte tausendmal um Verzeihung dass ich heute bei Ihnen nicht sein kann. Eine sehr wichtige Sache ist dazwischen gekommen.

Einige Nachrichten habe ich schon, aber die werde ich später mitteilen.

Wenn Sie gestatten, werde ich Ihnen morgen um 3 Uhr telefonieren.

Ihr Ergeb.
Nik. K—itch.

Meantime the spies remained at their post. The following morning Nicholas Karlovitch telephoned me to say that he could not come that day either, and at lunch time I noticed that the spies had left. Very shortly afterwards Mme. Schultz called with the news that I was to have been arrested that afternoon had we not communicated with the Chief of Staff, who had telephoned the Secret Police instructing them to find out about Nicholas Karlovitch and to have the spies arrested.

Then the "murder" was out. Nicholas Karlovitch turned out to be an agent of the Finnish Secret Police, who had taken me for a Bolshevik *provocateur*. And the affair ended with a severe reprimand to the police from the Chief of Staff. It was not until the episode was over that I realised how much it had begun to play upon my nerves.

The same day a message came from Russia to the effect that no more had been found out about Sidney.

I was now desperate. My mental balance was upset and I was far from normal. I begged my new friends to secure me a Bolshevik passport with which I could go into Russia and find my husband. Mme. Schultz was horrified at the thought. She said it was suicide. I knew it was suicide. But suicide was better than this, suicide was better than uncertainty, suicide was better than kicking my heels, suicide was better than waiting, waiting, waiting.

I believe I broke down. I called aloud for revenge. Something could be done, and if nobody else would do it, I would. And there I was, helpless in an indifferent world. Mme. Schultz stood over me, kind, capable, sensible, sympathetic. She asked me to trust her completely. I took her hand dumbly. She asked me to join the organisation. I trusted her. With the approval of the Moscow centre I joined the "Trust" under the party name of "Viardo".

And thus it was that I stepped into my husband's place in the ranks of anti-Bolshevism.

CHAPTER TWO

And then I think I went nearly mad. I was crazed with grief and suspense. My thoughts were gnawing at my heart like black serpents. The enacting of the Nicholas Karlovitch affair had buoyed me up for a time. And then it ended in an anti-climax, leaving me at a loose end and at liberty to brood, as the lack of news from Russia gave me ample occasion for doing.

No news from Russia. Marie Schultz tended me and watched over me during those dreadful days. It was a strange maelstrom which had drawn this capable, sensible, womanly woman, whom nature one would think had intended to be a governess in a respectable bourgeois family, into its ghastly and forbidding vortex. But Marie's appearance belied her. This calm, business-like, womanly woman, the daughter of a general in the old Russian army, had herself served as a trooper against the Germans. And now, her kindred done to death by the those same Red monsters who had taken Sidney, the indomitable Marie carried on her warfare against enemies of civilisation who had despoiled her native country and by their existence tainted the rest of the world. Marie comforted me. She had the gift. But I was almost beyond comfort. And then Marie swore that, come what might, she would bring my husband back to me. Henceforward her life would be devoted to that and that alone. All the work which she was doing for the "Trust" should give way to that: all the conspiracies in which she was engaged should go into abeyance, until she had lifted in some way the sorrow which she had been the means of bringing upon me. That would be her message to the "Trust".

"And they must find out for me," she said, "I am of the greatest value to the organisation, and they will adhere to the terms I make. I will turn my hand to nothing else, until I know what happened to Captain Reilly. I owe it to you, for it was at my instigation that Captain Reilly went into Russia. They must find out. Their influence penetrates into the governing circles of Soviet Russia. There is nothing which passes in the country of which they cannot know if they wish."

But when I asked who were the secret leaders of the "Trust", Marie was silent. These secrets were known only to a few, and woe to the member of the organisation who violated the confidence. Marie was fanatically loyal. Her belief in the "Trust" amounted almost to adoration. Her husband's position was quite inferior. He was "undoubtedly a very brave boy", as Sidney had said, and he proved a magnificent subordinate. But Marie's was the brain, which directed his coming and going. Poor George Nicholaivitch, he was very simple, very sympathetic, very anxious to help. I used to catch him looking at me with a sort of dumb sympathy in his eyes. But he could do nothing. He looked to Marie for orders. We both relied on Marie. And Marie, serene, bustling, capable, went on her way.

Still there came no news from Russia. Again I pressed Marie to secure me a Bolshevik passport, that I might cross the frontier and go in search of my husband.

"Useless at present," was Marie's reply. "You must learn the language first. Study the language. Yes, you must go into Russia sooner or later. As soon as you know the language sufficiently—*nous verrons.*"

And still there was no news, and I bethought me to play my second card. My plan was to publish in *The Times* the announcement of Sidney's death. Of course I did not then, and do not now, believe him dead, but such an announcement as I contemplated might lead the Bolsheviks to make a statement on their side. Moreover private affairs could no longer be held over, and some reason must be given why Sidney should not be attending to his business.

Marie agreed that the announcement might prove effective, but she asked me to wait until she had time to communicate with the Moscow centre and obtain their permission, as the publication might endanger their activities and the lives of the members of their organisation.

In Helsingfors as in London I was a caged lion.

I longed to do something, and there was nothing to do but wait. When I had first tried to buy help for my poor husband, I had used my knowledge of Z. and his poison gas. I have already mentioned how Z. was supposed to be in touch with a group of German monarchists, who had in their possession a new kind of poison gas more terrible than any ever known before. Z. had come to an agreement with the Germans, by which they would sell him the secret of this gas, for use against the Bolsheviks. The treachery of Savinkoff had put a stop to this project, but I remember that on the night before we left for America Z. had again asked my husband to go into the matter. That was the price, with which I bargained with the "Trust." If they would find out for me the truth about Sidney, I would try to get this gas for them.

Accordingly on a bitterly cold morning, I set sail for Stettin en route for Paris. Marie Schultz saw me off and took leave of me very tenderly. And before I went she promised once more that all her energies would be devoted to finding out what had happened to Sidney, and that she would leave no stone unturned in the quest. She would go at once to Moscow and confer with her superiors there. If they had no news she was to lay my scheme before them, and, if they approved of it, she was to send me a telegram "Signez Contrat." In the meantime I was to study Russian, and as soon as I was sufficiently proficient in that language, was to join Marie in Moscow. And I was also to bargain with Z. about the poison gas.

Well, in due course I arrived in Paris, a very different person from the one who left it. Now I was an anti-Bolshevist agent. For good or ill, for revenge and just to find out, I had made common cause with the people in whose service Sidney had gone to his mysterious doom, and for reasons which are sufficiently obvious, went to an obscure hotel and took a small room there. In the past few weeks my whole attitude towards life had changed. Previously I had been fond of pleasure and the good things of life; I would not willingly have hurt a fly: I had a great tenderness for all created things, and for the world which was so beautiful: I had successfully shut my eyes to the very existence of that insidious Eastern plague beneath the surface of it all. Now all that was changed. As I write now, I shudder to think of what I felt myself capable then, of what I might so easily have done in those terrible days. Only somebody, who has been through such a time can understand how a person might be guilty of a political assassination and call the crime a virtue and its retribution martyrdom. My family, to whom I now communicated the whole story, could not understand me at all, and urged me to break the connection and return to England. But I was ferociously determined. My first contact with this kind of life, the misery I saw everywhere, my own heart almost broken, the opposition of all my friends to the kind of life I

now intended to live all worked upon me, until I
was ripe for anything. And gradually the thoughts
of revenge wormed their way through and worked
uppermost in my mind.

At last the message came.

"Signez Contrat." I went to *The Times* office in
Paris and inserted my announcement.

"Sidney George Reilly killed September 28th
by G.P.U. troops at the village of Allekul,
Russia."

The announcement brought the following letter
from Dr. Williams.

DEAR MRS. REILLY,

We are grieved to hear the news and have been
thinking of you a great deal. My wife would have
written but she expected to hear from you from Paris
and I was surprised when the announcement came in
yesterday. Acting on the message from you through
our Paris office we, of course, published it at once, but
we have published as yet no comments as I was rather
waiting for the result of enquiries and certain political
complications might have been possible. In a day or
two I hope we may be able to say something. It is
surely very hard for you to find consolation at such a
moment, but, if there is any, it must be this, that he
died well and in the best of causes.

With kind regards, etc.,
HAROLD WILLIAMS.

And the next day of course all the organs of the
popular Press in England came out with their accounts of Captain Reilly's adventurous career in
the service of his country. It was understood that

the British Foreign Office was making an investigation.

However my little plan was not entirely successful. The Bolshevik papers contented themselves with acknowledging the truth of the story of Sidney's death. It was not until many months later that, following the death of Voikoff, they began to put about their horrible lies, saying that he had betrayed to them Mr. Churchill as the instigator of his mission.

I now had a little breathing space as far as my private affairs were concerned. And meanwhile Marie was busy getting at the truth of the whereabouts of Sidney. She wrote in a more optimistic vein. She had set all her powerful machinery in motion. The "Trust" would find out something. Meantime I must make progress with my Russian, and she would secure me the passport into Russia I so earnestly desired.

The first visitor to bring his condolences to my hotel was Z. The second was old Burtzev. Kindly, gentle old Burtzev, you would never recognise in him one of the foremost anarchists of his time. But so he was, and chief of the Revolutionary Secret Service at the time of the Empire.

The visit of Z. was particularly welcome, as it enabled me to put in train the plan which had brought me to Paris. Z. was very inquisitive. He very soon had asked me who were the people, on behalf of whom my husband had gone to Russia; and when I answered that they seemed to me to be very honest and trustworthy people and that I had joined them his interest knew no bounds.

After that Z. called on me frequently, and at last, having carefully prepared the ground, I broached the question of the poisonous gas. Z. affected diffidence, but his eagerness to get into touch with my principals was obvious. I then made my conditions.

If I brought him into contact with these people and they came to an arrangement with him, he must give me his word of honour that he would let me have a sample of the gas to give to the British Government without informing his German friends. I told him that I could not have a hand in such an arrangement, involving a weapon of war which might well be employed against my country without informing my government of it. Again Z. was diffident, but so eager was he to meet my principals that it is my belief that he would have accepted any terms. He only asked that I should never betray him.

Have I betrayed him by writing this confession? No. There was never anything to betray. Negotiations went on with Z. for nearly a year and nothing was done. Z. made excuse after excuse for delay. I believe to this day that his only reason for assenting to my terms was that he wished to be initiated into the secrets of the organisation for which I worked.

Well, he *was* initiated. He did meet one of the principals. Marie Schultz came from Petrograd to Paris and started negotiations. She came twice. She came a third time, bringing an expert with her. But Z. still made excuses and still held back.

I need not say how I questioned Marie every time she came. What *had* happened to Sidney? What *had* the "Trust" discovered? Surely they must know *something* now? But the answer was always, No, nothing. Poor Marie, I could see how her heart was bleeding for me. But *calm*, optimistic, busy, self-reliant, she went on her way. She was keeping faith. She was concentrating all her energies to finding out what had happened to Sidney.

Meanwhile Z. was whispering into my ear terrible things. Day after day he came to see me. Day after day his sinister suggestion sank into my mind. Day after day I fell more and more under his influence. And the things he said were terrible —and I believed him. I listened to him, horrified and fascinated. I was prepared to obey him. Oh, I know it sounds terrible in cold blood, this thing I nearly did. But *then*—it was different.

I was half-mad. I had been oppressed by a grief almost too great to bear. My mind swam in blood. The courage which sustained me was the courage of despair. And Z. was so cunning, so insidious. "Revenge," he whispered, always "Revenge". At that first terrible Christmas, following my bereavement, when I had returned to Paris alone, at my wits' end and not knowing what to do, he sent me his card with the following message.

"I can't wish you happy Xmas nor happy New Year but revenge, revenge, for my country, for the numberless victims, and for dear Sidney."

That was always his story. Revenge? Yes, that was my wish, but how to set about it? Z. had a practical idea, the idea, for which he had so assiduously prepared me. I could force the government to take action. I could bring my grief before the tribunal of the human race. And in helping Sidney, I could strike a shrewd blow at our enemies. How was it to be done? According to Z. it was the simplest thing in the world. All I had to achieve was a political assassination. There was absolutely no danger in it to myself. I would never be convicted in France if my story were told. He and his friends would arrange for my defence as they had done for that of Conradi in Switzerland. Rakovsky, the Soviet ambassador in Paris, was the victim, whom Z. chose for me.

And I, I was only too ready. Some such deed of violence rhymed with my thoughts at the moment. Anything, anything. This waiting was driving me mad. Something must be done. And thus I, a perfectly normal person who had led a perfectly normal life, and never taken a feverish interest in politics, almost joined the ranks of those fanatical martyrs, who use murder as a political weapon.

The thing, which saved Rakovsky and myself too was an accident of a nature which seems ridiculous enough in retrospect. When my mind was a blood-red blur and all my thoughts, sleeping and waking, were concentrated on revenge, when all was ready for my attempt, Z. sent me a copy of Shaw's *St. Joan*, which was, I suppose, to serve me as an example of martyrdom.

As I opened the volume there ran out from between the pages a loathsome insect. I dropped the book and sprang back with a shriek, and the insect fell to the floor and scurried away into a corner. It seemed to me like a warning, and at that moment I decided to put the matter to the priest, who was my confessor.

When I had come to Paris, the more completely to identify myself with the cause, for which Sidney had lost his liberty, and to which now I had devoted myself I had joined the Russian Orthodox Church. Marie had given me an introduction to a priest in Paris. This circumstance, by providing me with a friend and confidant in my loneliness, was to save me from the greatest misery and remorse.

The priest was horrified beyond words by the statement which I made to him. He said that in certain cases he quite saw the necessity of such actions, but such an act as that I thought of committing would not only be a sin but would help nobody. It would stain my conscience, it would endanger the life of my husband, and it would do unutterable harm to all the *émigrés*, who had found a home in France. And this ends the story of my career as a political assassin.

I returned to London and by the help of Captain

Hill and Sir Archibald Sinclair—who had been Mr. Churchill's secretary and closely connected with my husband's department—I interviewed Mr. Gregory at the Foreign Office. The British Government could take no action. The utmost they could do was to find out details of Sidney's death through their secret agents in Russia. There was no help. I wrote to Mr. Churchill, and received from his secretary the following letter.

22nd December 1927.

Dear Madam,

      Mr Churchill desires me to acknowledge the receipt of your letter of the 13th December, and to say that it appears to have been written under a complete misapprehension.

      Your husband did not go into Russia at the request of any British official, but he went there on his own private affairs.

      Mr Churchill much regrets that he is unable to help you in regard to this matter, because according to the latest reports which have been made public Mr Reilly met his death in Moscow after his arrest there.

Yours faithfully,

Emarsh

Mrs Reilly.

CHAPTER THREE

Still no news of Sidney. The days shortened to midwinter and lengthened out again in spring. Once more the winter stripped the trees, and a second time the spring clothed them in green. And all the time Marie worked unceasingly on the mission she had set herself—to find out what had happened to Sidney. But still there was no news. Marie came to Paris now and again, bustling and business-like as ever. Her husband too, George Nicholaivitch, I saw from time to time, when the missions on which Marie employed him brought him to the French capital and the Russian colony there. Marie's was the brain at the back of the scheme. The whole power, influence, intelligence of the "Trust" was being employed to find out the truth of what had happened to Sidney.

At the beginning of 1926 I received the following letter from the centre in Moscow.

DEAR MADAM,

Mme. Schultz has acquainted us with the contents of your letter and we are very touched by your frankness and by the fact that you are ready to help us in the work to which we have pledged ourselves.

The misfortune which has befallen you appears to us so great that it is impossible for us to find any words of consolation to express our feelings of sorrow. We

Mardi, le 29. XII. 1925.

Chère Madame,

Mme Marie Schoultz nous a fait savoir le contenu de votre lettre et nous sommes très touchés de votre franchise et de ce que vous soyez prête à nous aider dans l'œuvre, à laquelle nous nous sommes voués

Le malheur qui vous a frappé nous paraît si grand, qu'il nous est impossible de trouver des paroles de consolation pour exprimer nos sentiments douloureux. Nous pouvons seulement constater, que la haine envers nos ennemis commans nous lie à vous et force à unir nos efforts.

Le sort cruel a voulu, que votre mari, qui était notre ami sincère, ait péri, comme beaucoup d'autres de nos amis. Et quoique nous nous considérions tous condamnés à l'avance, nous continuons à lutter dans le ferme espoir que le bien triomphera du mal. Ne vous croyez donc pas, chère Madame, si solitaire. Sachez bien que vous avez des amis, — amis un peu lointains peut-

-être, mais des amis sincères, prêts a tout sacrifier pour vous et faire tout leur possible pour vous soutenir.

Veuillez croire, chère Madame, que la mort de votre mari sera vengée, mais dans ce but votre précieux concours nous est indispensable. C'est avec le plus vif intérêt que nous avons appris vos dessins et l'activité que vous déployez. Nous vous prions donc de continuer d'agir pour notre œuvre commune.

Quoique nous vous considérions déjà comme membre de notre grande famille nous sommes très heureux, Madame d'apprendre votre désir d'entrer au sein de l'église orthodoxe, ce qui nous unira encore davantage.

Il serait parfait, si vous pouviez apprendre un peu notre langue,—ce qui ne vous couterait pas beaucoup de peine: d'après ce que nous a dit Mme Schoultz, vous avez des capacités linguistiques étonnantes. Nous vous aurions priée alors de venir chez nous, afin que vous puissiez prendre part au travail actif et que nous vous présentions les membres de notre groupe. Nous pourrions vous prouver en même temps notre dévouement sincère et travailler avec vous dans le même but final.

Que Dieu vous vienne en aide dans votre douleur et vous donne une consolation dans le travail, que vous désirez partager avec nous.

Vos amis lointains

Klein

Levine

Padunotun

Ring

KLEIN AND LEVINE WERE NAMES ADOPTED BY JEKOFFLEFF AND OPPERPUT.
THE LATTER BETRAYED SAVINKOFF AND MARIE SCHULTZ

can only say that hatred of our common enemies binds us to you and compels us to unite our efforts.

Cruel fate has decided that your husband, who was our sincere friend, should perish like many others of our friends, and though we consider ourselves all doomed in advance we continue to fight in the firm hope that Good will triumph over Evil. Do not think then, dear Madam, that you are alone. Be assured that you have friends, friends a little distant perhaps but sincere friends, friends prepared to sacrifice everything for you and to do everything in their power to help you.

Please believe, dear Madam, that the death of your husband will be avenged, but to this end your valuable co-operation is indispensable to us. It is with the most lively interest that we have learned of your intentions and the activity which you are employing. We beg you, then, to continue the work for our common cause.

Although we regard you already a member of our great family, we are very happy, Madam, to learn of your desire to enter the fold of the orthodox church, a thing which will unite us even more.

It would be excellent, if you could learn our language a little, a thing which would not give you much trouble after what Mme. Schultz has told us of your astounding talents as a linguist. We should then ask you to come to us so that you could take an active part in the work and so that we could introduce you to the members of our group. We would be able at the same time to prove to you our sincere devotion and to work with you to the same final goal. May God come to your aid in your grief and give you consolation in the work which you desire to share with us.

Your distant friends,
KLEIN, LEVINE, KING.

The letter is written on lined paper in a vertical and rather undeveloped hand and bears three sig-

natures, none being in the same handwriting as that
of the writer of the letter. The names are of course
noms-de-guerre, and the very greatest secrecy was
maintained about the real identity of our heads in
Moscow. It was understood however that they
were all men of standing, and that one at least
held high office under the Bolsheviks.

Oh, if I had only known, if I had only known.
Klein stood for Jekoffleff, a high Bolshevik official,
and Levine was Opperput, Opperput the Russian
Iscariot, who had betrayed Savinkoff, who had
betrayed Sidney, who was to betray Marie Schultz,
when the "Trust" had exploited her enough. But
of course I knew nothing of this at the time. Not
yet had I reason to doubt the honesty and sincerity
of the organisation.

This was the only communication I received
direct from the heads of our organisation in Moscow. Their other instructions came to me through
Marie, and now and again an emissary of the organisation would visit me in Paris. They were very
insistent that I should learn the language and go
to Russia as soon as possible. Indeed Marie did not
wish me to wait until I had really mastered the
language, but advised me to secure a foreign passport as soon as I had a working knowledge of it.
One of the American republics at once occurred
to me, and I was successful in securing a false
passport from one of my friends in a South American Legation in London.

And meantime Marie was devoting her life to

finding out what had really happened to Sidney
Reilly. She wrote to me now from Moscow, now
from Petrograd, now from Helsingfors, now from
Warsaw. Her letters were very innocent on the face
of them, but they contained messages written in in-
visible ink, which I developed and read in Paris.
True to her promise she was leaving no stone unturned.

"What a woman," said George Nicholaivitch,
following her with adoring eyes. "She can do anything, anything. I give you my word, Madame
Pepita, my wife is the most wonderful woman on
earth."

One side of Marie's life remained a complete
mystery to me, that which concerned itself with
the heads of the organisation in Russia. Beyond
the fact that one at least was a highly placed Bolshevik official I knew nothing about them. Mysterious, masked figures they worked behind the
scenes of politics. Of course all the heads were in
Moscow. General K.'s relations with the "Trust"
were purely incidental. But his authority over all
the anti-Bolsheviks outside Russia was absolute.
When I told him of the message I had received
from the Moscow centre, and that I was busy
learning Russian so as to proceed to join them, his
orders were blunt and to the point.

"Don't go."

I remembered how he had given the same advice
to Sidney, and on the very night of my conversation with him I had a dream. I thought we were

back in our room in London, and Sidney came
and stood by my bed, saying, "Whatever you do,
however great the inducement held out to you,
however plausible those that ask you, never let
yourself be tempted into Russia." The words were
so clear, pronounced in his dear voice, that I
awakened with them still ringing in my physical
ear. I could still hear the echo of his well-remembered tones. It was some minutes before I realised
that he had not suddenly come back to me, and
had not actually been in my room and spoken to
me. When realisation came that it had only been
a dream and that I was in very deed alone, I broke
down and wept there in the darkness.

And Marie was then in Russia. Marie was in
the very jaws of the trap. Marie was in the utter-
most danger. I suddenly longed for her to come
back. I had grown very fond of Marie. I relied
very much on her, as did everybody else who came
into contact with that amazing woman. I was never
allowed to pierce the *arcana* of her Russian life.
The "Trust" was like a great lodge of Freema-
sonry, in which there were degrees of initiation,
and I was as yet a neophyte. I did not even know
the real names of the signatories of the letter I
had received from Moscow. If I had but known at
that time, I might have saved Marie from going
to the doom, to which she had already unwittingly
sent so many of the brave and the true.

Meantime I sought to ingratiate myself with my
chiefs in Moscow, so that they should put all their

efforts into the enquiry they were making for me. Various commissions reached me from time to time. Thus I was to obtain a poison, which would mix with food or drink without taste and would make people ill for a week without killing them. This, they explained, was needed to give the soldiers on the day when the "Trust" would make its final attempt to overthrow the Soviet *régime*. The instructions for me to secure a passport and go to Moscow became more and more pressing, but General K.'s counter instructions were uncompromising.

On another occasion I was asked to proceed to Warsaw, where a German paper manufacturer had succeeded in exactly counterfeiting Russian money. The motive of the scheme was to discredit and bankrupt the Bolshevik Government. I refused to have anything to do with the scheme, and the event proved that I was right. It is needless to recall how several prominent anti-Bolsheviks were drawn into the net, and suffered through being victimised by this insidious provocation.

But by now I was beginning to have doubts of the "Trust." I had been assigned so many ludicrous tasks, led up so many blind alleys. Moreover it was difficult to believe, if Marie were right in ascribing such powers to her chiefs, that they should after such a length of time still have failed to find out anything about Sidney. The most contradictory reports came through about him. Now I was positively assured that he was dead: now they told me that he was alive, and were certain that before long they would be able to trace his place of confinement.

Was it possible that there were traitors in the "Trust"? If news coming through to me was intentionally misleading, it pointed to traitors highly placed in the organisation.

When next Marie came to Paris I taxed her with my suspicions. I can see her now as she rose and walked up and down the room in anxiety and mental perturbation.

"Marie," I said to her, "promise me one thing, that you will not repeat my suspicions to your chiefs in Russia."

"No, no," cried Marie with a shudder, "I cannot give that promise. They must know everything. If anything occurs which makes you suspect, please do not tell me. Tell General K., but not me, not me."

"And why not you?"

"Because I must report it. You do not know the heads of the 'Trust'. Besides, we are bound by an oath—yes, we are bound by an oath."

Then I feared for Marie. I felt the cold fingers grip my heart. She was perturbed. She had doubts of her own. I knew it at that moment. I begged her to stay in Paris. I begged her not to return to Russia. Marie smiled calmly.

"I have promised you not to rest until I have found out what happened to Sidney," she told me.

Poor Maroussia! She returned to Russia, and

her letters began to get stranger and stranger. She seemed to be afraid of her own words. She wrote, one would think, under some restraint, as if some unseen watcher were peering over her shoulder. I was terrified. I had grown very fond of Marie. I ached for the time when she should come back to Paris. I felt that some hideous danger were impending over my dear friend in Russia. In peril of course I knew she was, but it was not the danger from the Bolsheviks I feared. Some frightful menace, obscene and hideous, sat beside her elbow as she wrote. And she knew it. I could see from her letters that she knew it.

At last to my infinite relief she returned to Paris. I need not say how overjoyed I was to see her. She was the last of my friends. But oh! What a different Maroussia it was that came back from Russia. Her eyes had a desperate, hunted look. Her face was worn and emaciated. Even her old self-reliance seemed to have broken down. Marie was afraid.

Of what? She tried to explain. She had left Russia contrary to the direct instructions of her chiefs, in order to put certain facts before General K. It was the act of insubordination which disturbed her. But I was not satisfied with her explanation. I was sure that she had discovered some act of treachery in the "Trust", and I put my suspicions directly to her.

Marie's denial was not nearly so confident as it had been before. She said that she did not think that there was actually any treachery. Her views did not quite coincide with those of her chiefs, that was all. She was all for action. She had managed to have a difference of opinion with them, and she was afraid they suspected her of double dealing.

"My coming here at all is an act of insubordination," she confessed, "and I must return to Moscow as soon as possible. When I said that I was going to Paris to confer with the General, they flatly ordered me to remain. My lodgings in Moscow were watched. I gave the watchers the slip and reached the station. A message was brought to me there to return. I disregarded it, and here I am."

"You will not go back to Russia," I said.

"I must, I must."

"Don't you think, Maroussia," I went on, "that the whole organisation might be a provocation on the part of the Bolsheviks, to enable them to get hold of all the counter movements, and to draw the anti-Bolsheviks into the net?"

"Oh no, no," cried Marie. "I have worked with the 'Trust' for over four years. In it are some of my oldest and most valued friends. For it I have pledged my honour again and again. It cannot be a provocation."

My mind went unhappily to the "Greens", the organisation of which Savinkoff had been the titular head. The "Greens" had been so called because they were supposedly a peasant party, neither "White" nor "Red". In actual fact they had been a provocation on the part of the Bolsheviks. A man called Opperput had played a large part in them.

As Marie was speaking I thought I detected a noise outside the door. I turned round and walked over to it quietly and as I advanced I heard foot-steps on the other side rapidly retreating. Nobody was in the passage when I opened the door. Our conversation had been overheard. Some spy unknown knew that Marie suspected the "Trust". If Marie returned to Russia she was doomed.

Marie had hardly time to confer with General K. when an urgent message arrived for her from Moscow, instructing her to return at once on a matter of the gravest importance, and she immediately prepared her departure. I was now thoroughly alarmed. Marie went to bid farewell to General K. and to receive his final instructions. His instructions were unexpected. He ordered her to stay in Paris.

But Paris was too far from the centre of those affairs which were all her life to Marie Schultz. Once again she was guilty of insubordination. The morning came and Marie was gone. I received a letter from her written on the train to Stettin. She told me that she was going to wait at Helsingfors subject to General K.'s permission.

And then from Helsingfors I received the following alarming letter.

MY DEAR PEPITA,

The catastrophe has arrived, all is lost, all is over, nothing remains but death. It is impossible to go on living with what I have just learned after four years' work during which I gave so much with so much joy. Now I know that all was false, that I was a dupe like so many others, that I have been fooled from day to day.

Our organisation was full of *provocateurs*, playing always the chief part and never giving opportunity to honest folks to penetrate to the bottom of our work. Whenever I wanted to clear up anything or to have an opinion of my own I was always accused of acting against discipline. And every time I smothered my doubts and submitted. But the moment has come, when one of those, who was taken by force and remained in their camp hypnotised by their omnipotence, has revolted and revealed everything to me. He has just escaped from Russia and now uncovers all the treachery, all the baseness of these people. You will read all this in the papers. You will know at last the truth of that, which has tormented us for so long a time. But my task is to carry my cross to the bitter end and confess all to you myself.

Your husband was killed in a cowardly and ignoble fashion. He never reached the frontier. All this comedy has been staged for the benefit of us others. He was captured at Moscow and imprisoned in the Loubianka for a month in the position of a privileged prisoner. Every day he was taken out for exercise in a car, and during one of these drives he was stabbed in the back by the order of the chief of the G.P.U.—Artanzoff, an old personal enemy of his, who thus took his revenge in this base manner. He was killed without conviction, without accusation, like a brigand. For the rest, the departure of Sidney Georgevitch to Petrograd, his journey to the frontier, the ambush at Allekul were all lies and acting. A volley was fired near the frontier, four persons were taken, were painted and carried like corpses to the station, where our agents saw them. An article was afterwards printed in the Soviet papers to the effect that four people were killed near the frontier of Finland.

The fact that I did not know does not diminish my responsibility. His blood is upon my hands, it will remain there all my life. I will wash them in avenging him in a terrible manner or dying in the attempt.

I dare say nothing to you, to whom I have brought so much unhappiness; I only want you to know that I shall not live if his blood is not avenged.

Always thine,

M.

P.S. I ask you one more favour: write to me under the name of S. All that you can find out in the letters bearing on the Savinkoff case about a man called Alexander Lepeliuz-Opperput. What part did he play in Savinkoff's past and what character is given him?

It must have been terrible for Marie to have the realisation forced upon her that for all these years she had been the dupe of the Soviet and that through her so many people, including the husband of her dearest friend, had been killed or captured, that the men with whom she had shared good fortune and ill, pleasure and peril, were traitors all and had been living a lie all these years.

As for the story about Sidney's death I simply did not believe it, and for the best of reasons. I had come into contact with some other people in Moscow in no way connected with the "Trust",

MARIE SCHULTZ'S LAST LETTER

rapport à l'affaire Sarinoff d'une
louaine qui se commit plusieurs
Speliez. Opperput Quel rôle a-t-il joué
dans L la partie de Sarinoff et quelle
caractéristique lui donne-t-on ?

who informed me that in December 1926 Sidney
Reilly was in the prison hospital of the Tcheka,
that he was not badly treated and that he was out
of his mind. The news came through somebody
in no way connected with any organisation, who
obtained it from one of the nurses in charge. Who
this person is I dare not reveal, as he is still in
Moscow. His last report was that Sidney had practically recovered and had been removed to another
hospital, where it was absolutely impossible for
him to get through to him.

The dangerous position of poor Maroussia
alarmed me terribly. Reading between the lines it
becomes obvious that her informant was the man
named Opperput to whom she refers in her post
script. Opperput was the man who had told her
all the lies about the death of my husband.

I did not need to refer to the Savinkoff papers
to give Maroussia a warning with regard to Opperput, whose treachery had been one of the most
marked features of the Savinkoff case. He had
been one of Savinkoff's Russian correspondents.
He had used the "Greens" as now he seemed to
have used the "Trust".

I sent Marie a telegram at once to the following
effect:

"Marie take no heed of all new lies. Distrust O.,
a person suspect and entirely without confidence.
Dossier follows in a few days."

And at the same time I posted to her an account
of Master Opperput's past activities, which would

have surprised the worthy gentleman had he known it.

However I received a reply from Marie dated 25-5-27.

MY DEAR PEPITA,

I have just received your letter, in which you report to me all the evil-doing of this man who was associated with us. Now I know all his past from his own lips—he has hidden nothing: he confirms many of the things that have been said of him: he states that he was forced by torture to tell all that he knew when he was taken prisoner in 1921, but he states in addition that he was never a *provocateur* before his arrest. Where the truth lies I don't know. Now he is unfolding everything, he is helping the representatives of the other countries who are being fooled and surrounded by Bolshevik agents to escape from this terrible position, and he is wrecking the result of five years' work of the G.P.U.

It is so easy to charge him with his past: all my soul revolts against him. But when I think that he is the only one of all those thousands and thousands, who has dared to revolt against his masters, who has had the strength to break through the hypnosis of their omnipotence, I feel that I shall behave like a coward if I turn my back on this man at this moment. You must fight against your enemy when he is strong and not when he has rendered himself of his own free will into your hands.

I do not wish to justify him, I do not wish to speak of his past which disgusts me but I have an idea which nothing can alter that we ought to give him the chance of rehabilitating himself by putting between himself and his past his blood or that of his masters. He says that is what he wants and I am going to put it to the

proof. If I am fooling myself again, so much the worse
for me. If I am right, we will acquire an ally who
knows them better than we do and who will always
find a means of over-reaching them.

All that he has told me so far about the duping of
the *états majors* and of the diplomats is absolutely
correct. There are plenty of proofs of it.

Who can be sure that he is not sincere? And if he
really is, he is a victim like all the rest.

Ask me nothing about my intentions: forget what I
have written to you at other times. Above all, speak
to nobody of my plans. By and by I will see you again
and then we will speak of all that.

I have sent you a telegram begging you to come
here. Now I think that it is better for me to come to
Paris. I want only to beg you to secure the publication
by your friends in *Liberté* of the articles which G.K.
will send on to you. The past of Opp. cannot prevent
us from profiting by the information which he has
given us. My advice is that we must do all in our power
to avert each of the ruses and basenesses, which the
Bolsheviks employ to fool and entrap honest people.

Understand that for me it is agony to speak of it:
I have suffered so much of it, but I have found the
power to forget my own sentiments and to cry out
their crimes against all the world.

Au revoir, ma petite, je t'embrasse tendrement, and
I beg you again to await me in Paris forgetting all I
have written to you.

Much had happened before this letter came into
my hands. Marie sent a telegram to General K.
announcing that she was returning to Russia. The
General wired back at once telling her to await
his arrival, and left for Finland with two officers.
He came back to Paris shaking his head and look-

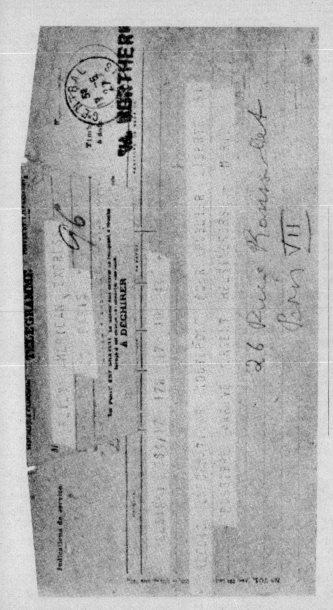

Telegram from Marie Schultz

ing very grave. He told me that the shock of the discovery which she had made seemed to have unhinged her mind and that she was no longer normal. She seemed bent on returning to Russia to wreak her vengeance on the people who had duped her, and thus to cleanse herself of the blood of the many, whom unwittingly she had sent to their death.

The General then left the two men with her and returned to Paris. A fortnight passed. And then one day at the American Express a telegram was handed to me. It had been handed in at Helsingfors and the date it bore was two weeks before. The clerk at the American Express apologised profusely. There was another Mrs. Reilly on their books and the telegram had been handed to her. On such things does human fate depend. The telegram was from Marie. She asked me to join her. She was going into Russia with Opperput, so great was the confidence with which this loathsome *provocateur* had inspired her. She wanted me to accompany her. In her grief and her loneliness her mind had flown to me, whom she had wounded so terribly and tried so hard to heal. Was there yet time? I wired Marie to await me, and hurried to the home of General K.

A terrible shock awaited me there. With the General were the two men, whom he had left at Helsingfors to watch over Marie. She had given them the slip and passed over into Russia with Opperput.

On the face of it, it is incredible. Marie, who knew the wiles of the Bolsheviks so well, had allowed herself to be lured into Russia by a transparent *provocateur*. Marie, who from bitter experience knew that there were no depths of duplicity to which the Bolsheviks would not descend, had been trapped by a device so patent as this. But there it is. One after another, the enemies of the Soviet were being lured back to their doom. No form of diabolical cunning in which the Bolsheviks were not past-masters. One way or another, with bluff and double bluff, they were drawing their enemies into the net. It is perhaps as Marie herself said that the omnipotence of the Bolsheviks exercised a sort of hypnotism, to which all became subject who approached the fringes of its baleful influence. How otherwise should these people, so shrewd, so well-informed, so sceptical, have been drawn into the lure?

Once the news reached us that Marie had gone back into Russia, it was only a matter of waiting for the news of her death. We had only a few days to wait before the papers published an account of how she had been taken by the Bolsheviks and, rather than be captured, had turned her revolver on herself and fatally wounded herself.

Opperput had escaped and had not been taken. Of course he had escaped. Of course he had not been taken.

And thus died the bravest of all Russian women, who fought against the tyrants of their country.

CHAPTER FOUR

And now the drama, in the course of which my husband had vanished and Marie Schultz had gone to an unknown fate, was drawing to its close. The terrible "Trust" had done its work of provocation mercilessly. First Sidney, and then Maroussia had fallen into the pit which had been dug for them. One had not even the consolation of knowing that they had died doing their duty. Fooled by a sham conspiracy, initiated into a bogus organisation, they had obeyed the instructions of their implacable enemies in going to a relentless doom. Life seems very vain and profitless.

But one victim was to die before the close. Immediately after receiving the news about Marie I had written to her husband—George Nicholaivitch Radkevitch, to give him his true name—a letter of condolence and deep commiseration. He was then in Warsaw. I shortly received the following reply in his poor, pathetic, misspelt, broken French.

DEAR MADAME PEPITA,

I thank you very much for your kind letter and I regret that I cannot send you any good news. The story is always sad and black.

I am writing to you, because I well know that you can understand me better than all the others. You have undergone the same suffering, and, what causes me infinite distress, your sorrow has come on you, without your will, through myself and Maroussia. You ought to hate us for that, but you have so much goodness that you pardon our fault.

God bless you for that, for otherwise existence would be entirely insupportable, and the only thing that would remain for me would be to die—for I do not see how I could possibly help you and make good the injury we have done. I am certain that it was for this reason that Marie put herself in that frightful position, where death was almost certain.

I did not see Marie for four months before that happened, but from her last letter I realise that she suffered terribly and wished to die.

You tell me that I ought to have a feeling whether Marie is alive or not. I think that it is impossible for me, particularly after what I have told you. I fear that my soul is not so sensitive as to receive impressions of what takes place on the border line or beyond the veil. Marie often used to tell me that I had a brain like a horse. I do not know if you can understand me: it is so difficult to explain in French, but I know that you will not laugh even if I make a mess of what I am saying.

I beg you to go to the fortune teller. Marie has told me how once she said a great deal that was true with regard to herself and Sidney Georgevitch. On one occasion to a man, who was a complete stranger, she named Marie and said that Marie would have to perish. I wanted very much to go to her myself but I have not the time for it. The same cause has prevented me from meeting you. Perhaps sometime in the future I will be in Paris, when I want to see you and explain what I cannot say in a letter.

You say that you are going to London to find out

something. I send you the last photograph of Maroussia. Take it with you. Perhaps it will help you.

Perhaps the others will laugh at my letter, but I know that you won't laugh, for you are good.

I want to tell you once again that I feel myself very blameworthy before you, and all the more I thank you for the interest you take in Marie.

It was not long before George Nicholaivitch followed his letter to Paris. His experience meantime had been terrible. At first he had been despairingly resigned to the blow. Then as time went on and he realised more clearly what had happened and that he would have to live without Marie for ever, his soul rose in revolt, and his hopes, overthrowing his reason, declared to him that Marie was still alive. He longed for company and for comfort. He was not the sort of man who can face life alone. Never have I seen a face so desperate. He was completely broken down. The sight of his sorrow-stricken countenance first, I think, drew me out of my morbid grieving for my husband, over whose doubtful fate I had been brooding all these months. I realised that there were others as wretched as myself and for a similar cause. George Nicholaivitch had relied on his wife as I had on Sidney. She had been his prop and stay. I have no doubt that she had ordered him to marry her as she ordered all the other activities of his life. He was not what you would call a strong character, only simple, loyal, kind-hearted.

I found him waiting in my room one morning

when I came down, sitting with staring, vacant eyes, with dishevelled hair, with drawn, desperate face. He looked as if he had had no sleep for nights, and as if he had been drinking too. There is something sacred in so much grief. I could say nothing. I had felt the death of Marie myself very keenly. I felt in a measure responsible for it. She had gone to avenge my husband, whom she had unwittingly betrayed. She had offered her blood for his blood by way of atonement. We had somehow been drawn into the vortex of horrible things, where death was piled on death, and fresh blood dripped on the old. So I sat and regarded George Nicholaivitch should go.

"Now Marie is gone," he said at last.

I said nothing. What could I say? I was acutely conscious of the clock ticking impertinently loud on the mantelpiece.

"Now Maroussia is gone," he repeated after a long pause. "But she will come back. She will come back."

"Of course she will come back," said I, to soothe him.

He laughed vacantly.

"Of course she will come back," he repeated. "I will go fetch her. I will go to Russia to fetch her.

"Wait and there will be news," I told him. "Wait here as I am waiting."

"Poor Mme. Reilly," he said, seeing me, it

seemed, for the first time. "You have been waiting a long time."

"A very long time."

"I cannot wait," said George Nicholaivitch. "I cannot wait a long time. I am going to Russia to fetch her. I cannot get on without her. I am going to-day."

"Stay a little in Paris."

"No, I must go at once." He started reaching for his hat. And then suddenly he turned round and looked me straight in the face. "*You* don't think she's dead?"

"I am sure she is not," I answered, to comfort him, though my own heart was like ice.

"That's right. Not dead. That's what I say. They say she's dead. They say she shot herself. But we know better. You and I know better—eh?"

"Of course we do," I answered.

"That's what I say. You and I know better. She's wounded. She's a prisoner. They have captured her and have her in prison. That's right, isn't it?"

"That's right," I assured him.

"Very well, then. Now what am I going to do? I am going to Russia and have her out. That's what I am going to do. Your husband is there too, isn't he? He's not dead, is he?"

"No, he's not dead either."

"Very well then. I am going to Russia and have him out. Have them both out. That's what I'm going to do."

I saw him later in the day in a café much frequented by Russian exiles. He was drowning his sorrows in drink. Without Marie to rule him and order him about, as that amazing woman did, poor George Nicholaivitch was going to pieces. But his desire to return to Russia remained unshaken. I asked him to stay and work with General K., but it was of no avail. Very worried, I sought out the general, and asked him to exercise his authority, but the General thought it better that George Nicholaivitch should go.

"You see what it is," said the General to me. "He is lost either way. If he stays here he just goes to waste and ends a gallant career in ignominy. It is better for him to die like a man in the open."

Of course George could not use his old passport. One day he came to me and asked me to get him another one. I was still diffident, but I had to admit the cogency of General K.'s reasoning.

Besides George Nicholaivitch himself was most pathetically serious and eager. After temporising a little I told him I would do my best.

It was from a Rumanian friend that I secured the false passport, which I gave to George, and now nothing stood in the way of his immediate departure. We lunched together at Drouan before he went, the General, George Nicholaivitch and myself. It was a queer meal. It seemed to me that poor Marie Schultz's husband was already dead. My heart was very heavy as I sat there and made a pretence of eating. Over the table General K.

gave his final instructions, as quietly and normally as if George Nicholaivitch was going out for a day's hunting. His first task was to find out whether Maroussia or Sidney was still alive: secondly, where they were confined: thirdly to get word to them: or, if that proved impossible, he was to blow up a part of the prison and endeavour to get at them during the confusion. But, before making any attempt, he was to inform the General and myself at two different addresses.

It seemed best that he should go, but God knows it was bitter to watch him depart to a certain doom. I wanted even then to call him back, but he went that afternoon, proceeding to Rumania and thence crossing into Russia, and the whole way the eyes of the trackers of blood were upon him.

With the exposure of the "Trust" my interest in Russian politics had waned. At the beginning of the year I had applied for a Bolshevik passport to enable me to go and see my husband in Russia. I had told the full story, keeping nothing back, and admitting that Captain Reilly had entered Russia under an assumed name on espionage work. But my request had been refused. However anxious they were to get me into Russia, the Tcheka did not wish me to enter the country thus openly. Any hopes I now had—and I am still convinced that my husband is alive in Russia—were centred in George Nicholaivitch.

The weeks went by. There was no news from George.

Then one morning there was a notice in the paper:

"EXPLOSION AT THE LOUBIANKA (MOSCOW)

"On the evening of July 6th two White Russian officers, who came from Paris through Rumania and Bulgaria, aided by Rumanian secret agents, threw two bombs in the Passport offices of the Tcheka. By the explosion one was killed and the other gravely injured. Mr. G. N. Radkevitch was killed, the other, an *émigré*, was arrested near Polosk (Moscow). A *communiqué* from Warsaw says that the Red Cross wagons have taken away many dead and wounded."

And so ended poor George Nicholaivitch Radkevitch, taking in his death a terrible revenge on the Tcheka, which had robbed him of all he held dear. About two months afterwards a letter reached me from Warsaw, written by him on the very day before his death and reading "trying to save both to-morrow. If I fail, adieu."

It was the report he was to send to the General and myself before he took action, according to the general's instructions. Were they both really still alive? Had George Nicholaivitch succeeded on his quest? Had he ascertained in what dungeon the victims of the Tcheka were lying? What happened to Sidney Reilly? Is he alive or dead? For my part I am sure that he is lying without trial or conviction in a Russian prison.

A memorial service was held for poor George Nicholaivitch in the Russian church in the Rue Crimée. It was for the third victim of the "Trust". As the priest from the altar pronounced the solemn and magnificent words promising immortal life to the soul of George Nicholaivitch Radkevitch, I saw their figures rise before me, saw them trailing up the shaft of summer light which shone through the window, saw Sidney and Madame Schovalovsky and Marie Schultz and George Nicholaivitch rising and soaring up the sunbeam into infinite space. My mind ranged over all the adventures which had befallen me in these few short years, I thought of the meeting at the Hotel Adlon, of our marriage, of Drebkoff, of Savinkoff, of what had happened to us in New York, Paris and London. I lived again through our parting on the platform at Cologne, and endured the agony of bereavement at Hamburg once more. The figures marshalled themselves before me and hurried into space. All that portion of my life seemed like a strange interlude, in which it was impossible to believe. And now I was quite alone. The sun had sunk to his setting; the streets were bathed in the religious gleams of evening; here and there lights were beginning to show in the windows, as I walked disconsolately home.

APPENDIX ONE

THE FATE OF BORIS SAVINKOFF

In his important "Methods of the Ogpu", Brunovski reproduces from the *Rul* the following article which he wrote on the fate of Savinkoff:

The most fantastic rumours have been circulated about, in which the truth is interwoven with the wildest fiction. To the realms of the latter must be relegated the assertion of Mr. Bulak-Bulachovitch that Savinkoff is alive. Savinkoff has been murdered by the G.P.U.

Murdered, not driven to suicide, as the G.P.U. was forced to assert.

Among my numerous "secret" prison correspondents were several leading Tchekists. This type of "correspondent", as will be readily believed, interested me above all others, and I always tried to get into touch with them, sometimes with the happiest results. As a rule, I made preliminary enquiries concerning the secret prisoners with whom I intended to establish connection.

Early in 1923, I was informed that cell No. 6 of the "death" corridor was occupied by a responsible employee of the Secret Operative Administration of the G.P.U., a man called Zapolsky, who was an active participant in the labours of the Polish Section of the Comintern. Naturally I mobilised every resource in order to get into touch with Zapolsky. I met with com-

plete success. I described myself as an Examining Mag-
istrate attached to the Trans-Caucasian G.P.U. I
found out that Zapolsky would undoubtedly be liqui-
dated and led him to believe that I too was a hopeless
"death" case. In other words, we soon became fast
"friends in distress."

This is what Zapolsky told me of the Savinkoff case.

B. V. Savinkoff stood at the parting of the ways. A
sudden change had occurred in his entire outlook. This
fearless revolutionary, ex-member of the Terrorist Section of the S.R. Party, friend and co-operator of Egor
Sozonov and Ivan Kaljaev, the moving spirit in the
execution of the Grand Duke Serge, Plehve and others,
could not settle down to a peaceful existence and decided to go to the U.S.S.R. for active collaboration
with the Bolsheviks. In 1923, and again in 1924, B.
Savinkoff entered into the secret negotiations with them
regarding terms. The conditions of the G.P.U. were
that he should visit the U.S.S.R., ostensibly of his own
free will and without the connivance of the G.P.U. His
public trial was to follow, at which his depositions
would embody sensational revelations. Savinkoff accepted all these conditions, declaring, however, that
he would make his disclosures not at the instance
of the G.P.U., but voluntarily. According to Zapolsky,
the G.P.U., nevertheless, succeeded in compelling Savinkoff in many respects to make his disclosures agree
with the aims of the Moscow rulers. Everything had
been arranged beforehand and an indictment had been
drawn up, hence events moved with relentless sequence.
On the 20th August, 1924, Savinkoff was arrested in
the U.S.S.R, on the 23rd he was handed a copy of his
indictment setting forth all his "crimes" against the
Workers' and Peasants' Republic and its Proletarian
Government. There were fully a dozen articles, each
one of which rendered him liable to be shot. Seventy-

two hours later his "trial" was held in the Military
Collegiate of the Supreme Court of the Union and at
dead of night of 24-25th August he was condemned to
death. Twelve hours later, professedly following a
resolution of the C.E.E. of the Union, his death sentence was commuted to ten years' imprisonment.

Savinkoff's true tragedy began after these events.
He was never granted his conditional liberty, although
he had an infinitely better time in the "Inner" prison
of the G. P. U. than the other captives: he was in receipt of an unlimited number of books, any papers he
pleased, including foreign ones, and was permitted a
daily motor drive through the town under the supervision of an escort. Yet this was not the life he had
dreamt of. As may be expected, his passionate, zealous
nature could never reconcile him with life in a Bolshevik dungeon. Savinkoff began to realise the trick
played on him by the Kremlin and Loubianka gang. A
number of letters, addressed to Dzerjinski, followed.
Savinkoff demanded the fulfilment of the agreement,
but alas! It is no easy matter to escape from a Bolshevik trap. Savinkoff's fate had been decided long
ago. Never, under any circumstances, did the Bolsheviks intend to allow him to go free.

Thus Savinkoff remained in the custody of the
G.P.U. It was not in the interest of the Tchekists to
be constantly bothered by his presence, particularly
after he had been fully utilised.

It was, therefore, decided to settle matters once and
for all. A suitable opportunity was all that was required and this soon presented itself. Savinkoff wrote
his famous letter addressed to Dzerjinski. After this
letter Savinkoff was poisoned and his corpse flung out
of the window of the office of the "Inner" prison situated on the fifth floor.

It was officially announced that Savinkoff had committed suicide and, by way of indirect proof, the letter to Dzerjinski was published in the papers.

This is the bare truth concerning the case of B. Savinkoff. The dust of time has settled over the deed itself, but it now bears eloquent testimony to the indelible vileness of these oppressors of the Russian nation, of Russian workmen and peasants.

APPENDIX TWO

WHAT HAPPENED TO SIDNEY REILLY?

The question of the fate of Sidney Reilly, which arises in the latter part of this book, remains as open to-day as it was six years ago. True to his rôle this man of mystery remains mysterious even in his passing.

The general idea in what are usually well-informed circles is that he reached Moscow, apparently undiscovered, and for proof there is the postcard which he sent from the Russian capital to Commander E. There he is said to have conferred with the Moscow heads of the "Trust" in a house in the outskirts of Moscow, and, when he had sufficiently incriminated himself, his companions revealed themselves as members of the dreaded Tcheka. The house had been surrounded. Every precaution had been taken to cope with the resource and courage of their arch-enemy. Forthwith he was taken for a ride in the American fashion and shot without further ceremony.

Such is the version of his end, which in default of further evidence, would pass for history. That he was dead before the end of 1925 is taken for granted, and the story of Brunovski is regarded with scepticism in official circles.

Brunovski's story first appeared in the Latvian paper *Segodnya* on September 26th, 1927, and is reprinted word for word in his book, *The Methods of the Ogpu*. It runs as follows:

BURIED ALIVE

Not long ago a Riga tailor in Blaumann Street, while overhauling my overcoat, which had spent four years with me in Moscow prisons, handed to me with an air of extreme bewilderment two strips of linen bearing strange, unintelligible inscriptions. I felt bound to explain the nature of these suspicious-looking fragments in the seams of my overcoat sleeve. The fact was that, having organised an extensive secret correspondence in prison with my fellow prisoners, I was compelled to enter memoranda in cipher on tiny fragments of linen and sew them up in various parts of my dress. On my arrival in Riga, I extracted my "mail," but completely overlooked the two notes.

One of these notes read: "British Officer Reilly. Persia. Father-in-Law." The reason for this entry was because in the first half of 1926 I learnt that an important British spy lay in the Butyrski Prison Hospital. He was isolated in a separate ward and only permitted walks under the supervision of two Tchekists specially appointed from the "Inner" prison to guard him. I was very anxious to get at the truth, and, if possible, to establish relations with the important spy. In this I failed completely, owing to the close watch kept over him. One of my secret correspondents was taken ill and had to be transferred to the Butyrski sick-room. I had reason to believe that he too would not be placed in a general ward. He was very clever and energetic, a wideawake sort of person, and I asked him to find out all he could regarding the British spy.

A few weeks later my friend left hospital and was put back in his cell. Our correspondence was renewed.

My friend also failed to get in touch with the Britisher. Nevertheless he did find out one or two things concerning him. As a result I made the above entry. At the moment I am quite unable to recall the meaning and reference of the words "Persia—Father-in-Law," but that is of secondary importance.

What is more important is this. In the first half of 1926 Captain George Reilly was still alive, and the Bolshevik version regarding his murder in 1925 is quite untrue.

What is the explanation? This is a difficult question to answer. One thing is certain: a communication of this nature was necessary to the Kremlin assassins. If Capt. Reilly is alive to this day, he is doubtless incarcerated in the "Inner" prison in one of the secret cells of "special designation."

These cells were erected in the loft of the "Inner" prison, and some captives have languished in them since 1918. These prisoners, registered under assumed names, are guarded by a special detachment of Tchekists. Every other day they are taken for a ten minutes' walk in the tiny prison yard near the prison baths and get their food from the Tchekists' mess.

Clearly they are life prisoners as long as Russia is ruled by the Bolsheviks. They are buried alive. If Captain Reilly is alive he is probably kept in one of these secret cells "till required."

In this communication there is a thing of the first interest which Brunovski relegates to a position of secondary importance. It is a thing of which he obviously knows nothing, and yet which stamps his story with the unmistakable seal of authenticity and veracity.

The words which puzzle him in the native Russian in which they were inscribed on the "tiny fragments of linen" are "Persia. Testi." So Brunovski read it in Riga. But he read it wrong. The last word was not the meaningless "Testi—Father-in-Law"—but "1 Esti."

And what is the significance of that? "1 Esti" was Reilly's secret name in the British Secret Service. Sidney Reilly had signed his last message, and signed it in a way which must prove enigmatic except to the very few.

INDEX

H

I

J

K

L